Additional Praise for
The Little Book of Alternative Investments

"In their *Little Book of Alternative Investments*, Ben Stein and Phil DeMuth bring their approachable style and wit to the investing world beyond stocks and bonds. For individual investors unfamiliar with the terminology and strategies of this part of the investing landscape, Stein and DeMuth provide an accessible overview, as well as suggesting ways that small investors can explore these realms. For everyone who has heard the hype and wondered what it all means, this book provides a readable and entertaining first step in coming to grips with alternative investment options."

—Geoff Considine,
Ph.D., Quantext

THE LITTLE BOOK

OF
ALTERNATIVE
INVESTMENTS

Little Book Big Profits Series

In the *Little Book Big Profits* series, the brightest icons in the financial world write on topics that range from tried-and-true investment strategies to tomorrow's new trends. Each book offers a unique perspective on investing, allowing the reader to pick and choose from the very best in investment advice today.

Books in the *Little Book Big Profits* series include:

The Little Book That Still Beats the Market by Joel Greenblatt
The Little Book of Value Investing by Christopher Browne
The Little Book of Common Sense Investing by John C. Bogle
The Little Book That Makes You Rich by Louis Navellier
The Little Book That Builds Wealth by Pat Dorsey
The Little Book That Saves Your Assets by David M. Darst
The Little Book of Bull Moves by Peter D. Schiff
The Little Book of Main Street Money by Jonathan Clements
The Little Book of Safe Money by Jason Zweig
The Little Book of Behavioral Investing by James Montier
The Little Book of Big Dividends by Charles B. Carlson
The Little Book of Bulletproof Investing by Ben Stein and Phil DeMuth
The Little Book of Commodity Investing by John R. Stephenson
The Little Book of Economics by Greg Ip
The Little Book of Sideways Markets by Vitaliy N. Katsenelson
The Little Book of Currency Trading by Kathy Lien
The Little Book of Valuation by Aswath Damodaran
The Little Book of Alternative Investments by Ben Stein and Phil DeMuth

THE LITTLE BOOK

OF

ALTERNATIVE INVESTMENTS

Reaping Rewards by Daring to Be Different

BEN STEIN
PHIL DEMUTH

WILEY

John Wiley & Sons, Inc.

Published by John Wiley & Sons, Inc., Hoboken, New Jersey.

Published simultaneously in Canada.

For general information on our other products and services or for technical support, please contact our Customer Care Department within the United States at (800) 762-2974, outside the United States at (317) 572-3993 or fax (317) 572-4002.

Wiley also publishes its books in a variety of electronic formats. Some content that appears in print may not be available in electronic books. For more information about Wiley products, visit our web site at www.wiley.com.

Library of Congress Cataloging-in-Publication Data:

Stein, Benjamin, 1944–
    The little book of alternative investments : reaping rewards by daring to be different / Ben Stein, Phil DeMuth.
        p. cm. – (Little books. big profits ; 31)
    ISBN 978-0-470-92004-6 (hardback); (cloth); 978-1-118-07524-1 (ebk);
    978-1-118-07525-8 (ebk); 978-1-118-07526-5 (ebk)
        1. Investments. 2. Portfolio management. 3. Asset allocation. 4. Investment analysis.
    I. DeMuth, Phil, 1950–   II. Title.
    HG4521.S7552   2011
    332.6–dc22

                                                                          2011002035

Printed in the United States of America

10 9 8 7 6 5 4 3 2 1

For every man and woman
who wears the uniform.

Contents

Introduction

_~_

Are You Alternative? Dare to Expose Yourself

LET'S TALK ABOUT YOU.

Be honest—you're tired of the same old up-and-down from your "missionary position" 60/40 stock and bond portfolio. You read about people who are experimenting with alternatives, and wonder—should you do it, too? Can it be wrong, if all the cool kids are doing it? Especially, the _rich_ cool kids? Certainly you don't want to get hurt, and you don't want to hurt anyone else. But you're curious. You've felt the attraction, and even though you've tried to fight it, it's not letting you go.

If you wanted to give the alternative investing lifestyle a spin, where would you start? Most of these investments are complicated and confusing, especially if you skipped graduate school that year. Meanwhile, the managers who specialize in them all talk to each other but rarely to outsiders. By law, hedge funds aren't even allowed to advertise, so they don't have a massive advertising budget devoted to reaching out and educating the high-net-worth about features and benefits. It's like you have to know somebody to get in.

Curious? That's where *The Little Book of Alternative Investing* comes in. Consider this little book to be your personal how-to *Kama Sutra* investment manual. We are going to rip off the plain brown wrapper and show you some new positions to try. We're going to take you on a tour through these strange and luxuriant jungle offerings, explain in plain English how they work, and tell you how to use them in the privacy of your own portfolio. We're going to take you for a walk on the wild side in a world where deviations are standard and returns are total.

All set? Strap yourself in, hang on tight, and get ready for the ride of your life.

Not So Fast . . .

Before you turn to the centerfold, you are going to have to wade through some pages of our *Playboy* investing philosophy. That way you'll know what you're looking at when you get to the pictures (or, in our case, charts).

What are alternative investments, anyway? By alternative investments, we mean alternatives to all those other investments that lose money, like stocks and bonds and real estate. In case you've been living in an igloo, you may have noticed that in the past decade or so we've had a stock bubble and then the popping of that bubble. Then everyone fled into the safety of real estate, creating a bubble that was followed by the popping of that bubble. Lately everyone has piled into the (supposed) safety of bonds until there's something going on there that looks for all the world like it might be a bubble (which would make for a trifecta undreamed of even by Bazooka Joe) but who knows? In other words, the three little pigs have run from one collapsing house to the next in an effort to keep the wolf from their doors. The quest continues for alternatives: something that's not a stock or a bond or a house that won't blow down. That's still pretty broad, though. For example, you might buy a hot dog stand. Is that an alternative investment? Perhaps, but it sounds like a pretty silly one.

Here your authors have caught a break. It turns out that there is no agreement on what "alternative investments" really are, so we are going to expose you to a bunch of them. Assets that are alternatives to stocks and houses and bonds might include other kinds of real estate, commodities, options, currencies, collectibles, convertible bonds, emerging market debt, and so on. More on these in due course.

In addition to these alternative kinds of assets, there are also alternative kinds of trading methods. These can also count as alternatives, even when they are using ordinary stocks and bonds. For example, you may have heard the expression "Sell in May and go away," a strategy that has worked in the stock market every single year in the past century except the years when it hasn't. Well, a daring alternative investor might go against the grain by buying in May and then sticking around. He might figure that all the selling pressure from price-insensitive investors anxious to get out of town in May could create a buying opportunity. Then he would sell the stocks back to these same investors in September, when their rush to get back into the market would bid up prices.

Actually, an alternative investor would do nothing of the sort, but you get the idea. In real life he is more likely to use strategies like hedging and shorting, which we will get into later.

The point is, because these alternative approaches are either buying different assets or using some novel trading method, the returns from investing in them should be different from investing in stocks and bonds. After all, if the returns from alternative investing were just like the returns from the stock market or the bond market, it wouldn't be much of an alternative, now, would it?

They Are the Eggmen

Since Stein and DeMuth believe in giving the investing public solid value for their reading dollar, we are going to sprinkle this book with some fancy finance vocabulary that you can throw around with no very great precision—just as they do on business TV. (Use these terms often enough and you may even get your own show.) We mention this to sugar-coat the fact that you may have to latch on to some new lingo to understand these investments. You will need to wrap the rubber band in your brain around a few ideas not already in your mental gym bag. Like possibly: *correlation*.

Correlation is the extent to which two things vary together. This relationship can be quantified and expressed by a number ranging from –1 to +1. If two things have a correlation of +1, they move in perfect lockstep with each other. If they have a correlation of –1, one will be up while the other is down. If they have no correlation, they move independently. For example, there is probably a high correlation between people who are politically liberal and viewers of MSNBC news. There is probably negative correlation between people who are politically liberal and regular viewers of FOX

News. But there is probably no meaningful correlation between political orientation and people who watch NBA basketball.

If you compare them side by side, stocks and bonds usually have a small or negative correlation to each other, which is why they are such good partners in an investment portfolio. On the other hand, most stock investments have fairly high intercorrelations, which is why they all tend to rise and fall as one. In a way, you might say that this is a book about our relentless quest to fill our portfolio with low-correlating assets.

What makes finding sources of uncorrelated returns so important? The answer is in two words: controlling risk. When you combine assets that don't correlate with each other in a portfolio, you get the average of all the returns but with *less* than the average risk of each investment taken separately. Some of the risk cancels out, because one investment is going up while another is going down. The less correlated the investments are, the more the individual risks negate each other so you get the same returns for less risk, at least usually.

For example, let's say you held a portfolio that was invested 60 percent in the S&P 500 Index of U.S. large company stocks and 40 percent in the total U.S. bond market for the years 1976 through 2010. According to Phil's infallible calculations, the stock side would have returned an average of 11 percent per year, the bond side would have returned an average of 8.4 percent per year, and the overall portfolio would have returned about 10.3 percent, roughly the weighted average of these returns.

What about the risks? The volatility of the stock side would have been 15.4 percent annually, the bond side, 5.7 percent annually. But for the whole portfolio? 10 percent. Which is less than the 11.5 percent that we expected when we combined them in a 60/40 weighting. That drop of 1.5 percentage points amounts to a 13 percent reduction in portfolio risk. We got it for free, through the magic of diversification. Harry Markowitz pointed this out in 1952 and ended up collecting a Nobel Prize for his insight, which became the foundation of Modern Portfolio Theory. Later on, Ben's economics professor at Yale, James Tobin, said that his 1981 Nobel Prize was for an elaboration on this one idea: Don't put all your eggs in one basket.

Why is it so great to get the same returns with less risk—so great that it wins economists a couple of round-trip tickets to Stockholm? Let's say in 2008 our investments fell 50 percent. Well, that's quite a hole we've gotten ourselves into. Now our investments have to go up 100 percent just to get us back to where we started. It's going to be a long, miserable slog. It will take years—years we don't have if we are close to retirement.

But . . . what if, through the magic of better portfolio diversification, our investments only fell 25 percent that year—if we dare use the word *only* in connection with *fell 25 percent*. Now we only have to get back 33 percent to return to the starting line. That is no picnic, but it is a lot better than the Bataan death march to make up 100 percent. Especially if it didn't cost us anything to get these better returns in the first place, because we got them through the free lunch of portfolio diversification by the expedient of using lower-correlated, alternative assets. Low correlation is what puts the disco in diversification.

Yet, commentators are always grousing about how the liquidity panic of 2008 showed the failure of diversification. This is precisely wrong. 2008 showcased the failure to diversify enough. We had plenty of pseudo-diversification but not enough of the real thing. Almost no one came away with their wallets whole that year—least of all your authors—but the fact that uncorrelated assets (apart from Treasury bonds) were hard to find does not mean that diversification itself failed. It was said that correlations "went to 1," but that is an overstatement. Certainly they went up, and virtually all risky assets lost

—— ⁓ ——

Low correlation puts the disco in diversification.

money. What really failed was the implementation of a strategy that was itself fundamentally correct and, if anything, should have been heeded more closely. Investors needed—and still need—radical diversification.

~

Commentators are always grousing about how the liquidity panic of 2008 showed the failure of diversification. This is precisely wrong. 2008 showcased the failure to diversify enough.

Of course, low correlation isn't everything. There's one more thing that alternative investments need to do to get our attention: They need to make money. Not every year, not all the time, but on average they need to produce a positive return. Otherwise they would just be adding sawdust to our portfolios. If they make money and have a low correlation to our traditional investments, they are going to diversify us into better risk-adjusted returns. We'll make more money faster and have a smoother ride getting there. This is the tantalizing prospect we dangle before you.

The Road to Millionaire Acres

Wall Street is forever manufacturing new investment products to sell to its customers. Lately, "alternative investments" have been big, capturing inflows of $18.8 billion in 2010. They have reached a critical mass and it is time to step back and survey the field. These products are relatively new and untested, so they deserve to be approached with skepticism. Are they just overpriced gimmicks? Which ones, if any, merit serious consideration?

We went out on the lot and kicked the tires. We asked questions: What is the secret X-factor behind the alternative returns—how does it make money? Is it reliable? Will the returns persist? How risky is the strategy? How expensive is it? Does it add value when parked alongside more conventional investments? How much should we use and what kind of results can we expect when we do?

This *Little Book* is going to answer these questions. We're going to name names and give you specifics. We're going to keep the weaseling and the bland generalities to the minimum daily legal requirement.

Here's what your authors have cooking.

First, we are going to pose a new way to think about your investments. This alone is worth the price of admission. It's going to show you what your portfolio has really been up to all along and why you've (probably) gotten hurt so badly in the past.

Then, we are going to hold up an X-ray machine to your stock and bond holdings, the way academic researchers look at them. We are going to suggest how to maximize your risk-adjusted returns from your conventional investments.

After that, we move to alternatives. We'll start with the *faux* alternatives like collectibles and private equity. Next, we'll talk about the conventional alternatives: commodities and real estate. Then we'll consider hedge fund strategies, which are the meat and potatoes of this book.

Finally, we will pull together our recommendations and suggest how you can put together a portfolio made of brick that combines your traditional investments with some new alternatives, adding growth potential and minimizing risk.

■ ■ ■

To put it another way, it has been observed that polygamy is a crime that is its own punishment. However, the opposite is true when it comes to investing. You want to have your lawfully married wife—the 60/40 portfolio, as it were—but then you want to have as many mistresses as you can, in the form of diversifying, uncorrelated assets. Sure, the 60/40 will be jealous that you are spending your money elsewhere, but you will be happier and richer as a result. We're not going to ask you to divorce your old portfolio. Far from it. As a horseman might say, it's going to be rode hard and put away wet.

The Alternative Reality

You are traveling through another dimension, not only of sight and sound but of money, whose boundaries are that of your bank account. That's the signpost up ahead—your next stop, *The Little Book of Alternative Investments*!

Chapter One

Everything You Know Is Wrong

Classify Your Investments the Alternative Way

THERE IS NO POINT CHASING AFTER ALTERNATIVES WHILE our conventional portfolio sits there like a broken-down wreck at the side of the road. After all, our conventional portfolio is going to be the source of most of our returns. It needs to be tuned up and purring like a cat. Only then can we use it to cruise around town and pick up alternatives.

Our conventional portfolio is invariably summarized by a pie chart. Everyone loves the look of a portfolio pie. You see them in books. You see them on the Internet. You see them on your brokerage statements.

These pie charts show how our assets are invested. Each wedge is a different color. U.S. stocks might be in blue. Bonds might be in red. Emerging market stocks in yellow.

A really colorful pie chart will divide your assets into many subcategories, each one getting its own special color: Large-Cap Growth Stocks, Large-Cap Value Stocks, Municipal Bonds, Treasury Bonds, and so on. We inserted one as Figure 1.1 for your entertainment. Unfortunately, we aren't allowed to use full-color graphics, so you'll have to use your imagination to get the full effect. (We suggested including 3D goggles to make it really pop out, but they shot down that idea, too.)

As exciting as these charts are, they can be extremely misleading. This is because when you see a whole box of crayons used to color in the different wedges of the pie, you might naturally assume that you own a nicely diversified portfolio. Unfortunately, many of these different wedges perform in about the same way—and never do they behave more in the same way than when Wall Street is self-defenestrating. It would be like someone who owned 16 different CDs by Yanni claiming he had a diversified music collection. While no doubt there are subtle

Figure 1.1   A Portfolio Pie Chart

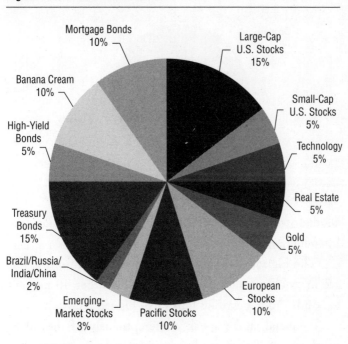

differences within the Yanni oeuvre, to many of us it sounds pretty much the same.

It is closer to the truth to say that there are really just two big wedges represented in your portfolio: a big wedge of stocks, and a big wedge of bonds or cash. This is the canonical 60/40 stock/bond policy portfolio, as widely dismissed as it is widely held, whose returns we just

Figure 1.2   The 60/40 Portfolio

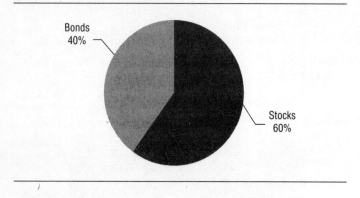

alluded to in the Introduction (you didn't skip the Introduction, did you?).

The big idea is that roughly 60 percent of our assets are in stocks of various colors, and the other 40 percent in bonds. Your portfolio looks like Figure 1.2.

Financial snobs speak contemptuously of the 60/40 portfolio, as if the people who own it don't know which fork to use at a dinner party. Your authors, however, love the 60/40 portfolio. It is a sensational portfolio for almost everyone, combining a bracing dose of caffeine from the stocks with a judicious modicum of port from the bonds. The fact that it is found everywhere should not blind us to its inherent beauty.

A portfolio can be 60/40 even if it is dressed up with a lot of sub-asset classes. In fact, this is probably a lot

like what you own right now. Or, maybe you own a portfolio that's 50/50, or 70/30. You get the idea.

While the 60/40 portfolio is undoubtedly great, that
is not to say that it is perfect. Like everything else, it has
issues. Issues that can lead to tissues.

What's wrong with the 60/40 pie? It implies that your
investments are pretty evenly balanced. That is false.
Stocks are about three to four times riskier than bonds.
The risks of the 60/40 portfolio are really allocated more
like those in Figure 1.3.

As you can see, almost all the risk in the 60/40 stock/
bond portfolio (85 percent; some say more) comes from
the stock side. The 60/40 portfolio looks like it is standing on two legs, when it's mostly standing on one: stocks.
This explains why when stocks hit a nail, the whole thing

Figure 1.3   The 60/40 Portfolio by Risk

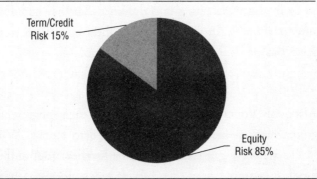

Term/Credit
Risk 15%

Equity
Risk 85%

goes flat. The 60/40 portfolio really acts too much like a stock portfolio, not a stock + bond portfolio. Even a good year in bonds will be overwhelmed by a bad year in equities. You might have a few ducks and chickens, but nothing else is going to make much difference with an 800-pound equity gorilla sitting at the center. Of course, even if stocks go to zero, you won't lose more than the 60 percent that you put into stocks to begin with—unless the bonds crumble at the same time.

The 60/40 stock and bond portfolio looks like it is standing on two legs, when it's mostly standing on one: stocks.

This goes a long way towards explaining why 2008 was such a disaster for investors. They were hypnotized by their pretty pie charts into thinking that they had diversified risk away. In fact, nearly all their eggs were in the same basket.

Addicted to Stocks

Although Robert Palmer never put it in a song, you're gonna have to face it—you're addicted to stocks. When stocks are on a tear there is nothing lovelier. Your authors fondly remember going for bicycle rides along the beach in Santa Monica during the dot-com era while their stock portfolios effortlessly climbed hundreds of points day after day. It was a great way to make a living. We thought we were rich.

While it lasted.

Lots of things in life are thrilling. But in the end, you have to ask: Can I afford them? As great as stocks are on the upside, they are sickening on the downside. With two major crashes in the last decade sticking out like an ad for a Playtex Cross Your Heart bra, you'd think we would have learned our lesson. That's just part of the story. A growing number of economists believe that stock market returns going forward are not going to be as vigorous as they have been since, say, the end of World War II. Some cite low dividends, some cite a declining rate of productivity, and some cite the overextended nanny state, but to these swamis the stock market's long-term historical return of 7 percent after inflation no longer seems bankable. Against this, we can't think of any mainstream economists offhand who are expecting future long-term returns from the stock market to exceed their historical averages. If this view is correct, the implications for the retiring baby boomers are tragic. Our best investing years would lie behind us.

Who knows? Not us, that's for sure. But that's not the end of it.

The problem we see is that almost everything else in your life is closely linked to the stock market, because the stock market is closely linked to the overall economy. Your job—and your spouse's job—for starters. When the economy is doing well, you are getting raises, promotions, the world is your oyster. Once a recession arrives, though, it's time for layoffs and cutbacks. Work becomes like death row—who will get the ax next? When there is a recession, you cannot waltz across the street to your competitor. They are laying people off, too. Even if you hang on by your fingernails, it is going to be stressful, and the stress will ricochet throughout your life and your family's life. Meanwhile, your working spouse will be going through the same grinder. Life may look different on one paycheck or half a paycheck, and it definitely will look a lot different on no paycheck.

What else is happening at the same time? Your 401(k) plan is going through the shredder. So is your company stock. Your stock options might become worthless. Your investment accounts—loaded with stock—are down and leave you with two bad choices: Take greater risk by selling your bonds (if any), or sell your stocks when they are beaten down, which is equivalent to a farmer eating his cow.

At the same time, the housing market is a graveyard. It can take a long time to sell a house in the middle of a recession, which is naturally a terrible time to sell. Being forced to sell your home just to climb out of debt is a very stressful prospect. In short, everything in your life is going to be circling the drain at the same time.

Our point is: Whether we realize it or not, most of us are wired to the stock market's electrodes more than we should be. It is great fun to watch stocks race up when the economy is strong, but it is a zing that many of us cannot afford to the degree that we do. Unless we work for the government or some bulletproof company that makes money no matter how the economy is faring (and there aren't many of those), we probably owe it to ourselves to lighten up on equities. Recessions happen, and when they do, the stock market suffers terribly.

But let us go back. . . . Why do we love stocks so much? Because we are greedy, naturally. The headline for stocks is, "Big Returns Here." In fact, our money chases whatever has offered big returns lately: stocks, houses, gold, whatever. Instead of chasing after kicks on Route 66, the sadder-but-wiser investor focuses on factors within his control: investment expenses, asset allocation (diversification), and risk management.

This book is largely about finding legitimate assets that will make your finances less tied to the churn of the stock market. To the extent that you succeed, the trade-off is that you really will be less tied to the stock market.

When stocks are rocketing to the stars, you won't be. When stocks are melting through the earth, you won't be. It will be less clear to you from day-to-day how you are doing. This can be liberating but also can be anxiety producing, especially if you're used to checking the Dow Jones Industrial Average every 15 minutes or 15 seconds. It requires a leap of faith that there is life beyond stocks. We want to interest you in accepting a higher degree of stock market de-correlation into your life than you probably have at present.

One very basic step on the road to recovery from stock fever is for most of us to hold more cash. This cash should be in some liquid form where we can get at it to buy gas and groceries, not locked inside a five-year CD at a bank in Sioux City. We are thinking money market fund, even if (as of this writing) they pay next to nothing in interest. We recently talked to an investor with $20 million in the stock market. Did he bail out in 2008? No. Why not? Because he had $2 million sitting in Fidelity money market funds. That cash was like a security blanket. It let him sleep nights without succumbing to panic. We need enough ready cash to get us through the next recession without trashing our future with a gigantic, lifetime-financial-returns-destroying "sell low" stock transaction.

Get more cash. It is an obvious but brilliant first step. Cash is the premier alternative investment.

~

Cash is the premier alternative investment.

Bye Bye Miss Portfolio Pie

If classifying your assets according to the amount of money you have invested in each of your holdings is devilishly misleading, what is the alternative? Instead of classifying your investments by *dollars* as the standard pie chart does, it is more useful to classify them by the *risks* to which those dollars expose you. This is a game changer. It will show you what you are really doing with your investments, whether you realize it or not. Looked at this way, you can immediately see if you are asking for trouble by having all your risk eggs in the same basket.

In finance, risk and reward are closely related. Over long periods of time, markets reward investors for taking certain risks. When investors put their capital at risk, they expect to be paid for it—whether they lend it to the government or buy shares of a publicly-traded company. Not all risks are equally rewarded, though. Putting all of your life savings on "00" at the roulette table would be a reckless risk, for example.

How do we chart portfolio risk? First, we have to measure the riskiness of each asset class. We equate risk here with *standard deviation*—a statistical measure of how volatile the asset class's price is. The higher the standard deviation, the more the price jumps around. The stock market has an average return of about 10 percent a year, with a standard deviation of about 15 percent. By definition, this means that, two-thirds of the time, stock returns will vary from minus 5 percent (the average return of 10 percent minus one standard deviation of 15 percent) to plus 25 percent (the average return of 10 percent plus one standard deviation of 15 percent). Once we know the standard deviation, we can even take a stab at predicting the probable upper and lower range of an asset class's price movements. This is not to be confused with how much you will lose when the market falls badly, which invariably proves to be many times greater. However, it is directionally correct. For all the complaints about standard deviation as a measure of risk, no one seems to have put up any better idea.

Once we know the standard deviation, we multiply the dollars we have invested in each asset class by its standard deviation and its correlation to each of the others, and voila, we can see the risk allocation of the total portfolio. Just for fun, Phil will post a spreadsheet on his web site so that you can play with this to your heart's content (www.phildemuth.com/pages/risk.htm).

Consider: Stocks have a standard deviation of about 15 percent, and bonds have a standard deviation of about

5 percent. Right away you can intuit that to balance these risks you would need a portfolio that has at least three times as many bonds as it has stocks, or in other words allocated with 25 percent of the money in stocks and 75 percent invested in bonds (see Figure 1.4). This is roughly the opposite of the 60/40 portfolio that most of us hold. There is trouble in paradise, however. Stocks have higher expected returns (say, 10 percent) than bonds (say, 5 percent). When we lower our allocation to equities, we also lower our expected returns. But we need the big returns if we ever want to retire. We have hit a wall.

Or, have we . . . ?

There are several ways to address this problem.

One way would be to *use leverage*: borrow money to amplify the returns of the more stable 25/75 portfolio.

Figure 1.4   A More Risk-Balanced Stock and Bond Portfolio

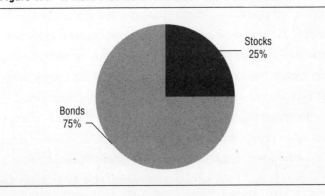

We're not talking about levering up 70-to-1 as Long Term Capital Management did before their hedge fund blew up. We would only jack up the returns to where they would have been if we had continued operating at 60/40—in this case, about 1.4-to-1. In other words, we would put up $100 of our own money, then borrow another $40 from our broker, and spend the $140 buying a portfolio of 25 percent stocks and 75 percent bonds. Magically, the resulting portfolio should deliver about the same returns with less risk than if we had stayed at 60/40 all along. In this scenario, we have swapped some of the equity risk for bond risk and added some leverage risk, spreading our risks around. While this approach is perfectly rational, we don't recommend it unless you have cheap access to capital and are more sophisticated investors than we are.

Another approach to solving this problem would be to *use riskier bonds*—bonds that, due to their long maturities or questionable credit quality—are just as risky as stocks. As we go to press, bonds appear to be extremely expensive, so we would shrink from this approach. We don't want to charge you with the job of monitoring interest rate curves and credit spreads on an ongoing basis.

Fortunately, there is another way. We can change our asset mix. We can add some new, low-correlating *alternative* asset classes that have higher expected returns than bonds do. That is what the rest of this book is going to be about. Then, in the last chapter, we will show you how to combine the new alternatives with your conventional portfolio.

The Alternative Reality

Instead of classifying your investments by how many dollars you have in each one, it is more revealing to look at how much you are exposed to the underlying risk factors that are driving your returns. Most investors are overexposed to one risk factor, equity risk, and would be safer spreading the risks around. Diversifying your dollars without diversifying your risks is just whistling in the wind.

Chapter Two

Efficient Market Theory and Its Discontents

Out with the Old, In with the New—Overhauling the 60/40 Portfolio

BEFORE WE DIVE INTO OUR ALTERNATIVE WORLD, we first want to talk about ways to tune up your basic stock and bond portfolio so you are maximizing the expected return for the risks you are taking. If you are like most people, your current portfolio would get comments from the teacher like "Needs work" or "Not working up to abilities."

Example: Your authors were having lunch at Nonna in Beverly Hills, when a man we had never met comes up to the table clutching a thick envelope from a well-known brokerage firm. Introducing himself, he pulls out his statement—about 50 pages long—and asks us what we think of his portfolio. This is the equivalent of the free curbside consultation that doctors are subjected to, now transplanted to finance. We asked him what he does for a living. He's a business executive and has an M.B.A. from Stanford. If this guy can't figure out his brokerage statements, what chance do the rest of us have?

Thumbing through the statement, we find page after page of stocks. Abbott Labs . . . Abercrombie & Fitch . . . Altria . . . and so on, down the alphabet. What do we say? Do we opine about each ticker, pro and con?

No. Not necessary.

Right away, we know that this guy is following the strategy of individual stock picking, one that seldom provides the best returns. It comes as no surprise that even by holding each page up to the light we can find no reporting anywhere of his returns, let alone of how those returns compare to standard market benchmarks. It is almost as if his high-priced brokerage was deliberately trying to snow him with data while withholding the very information he would need to make an intelligent decision about the course of his investing.

There are a lot of investors out there in his position. They are paying 1 or 2 percent every year in fees for a "wrap" account, but they have little idea how they are really doing.

This brings us to the key, life-changing insight from Vanguard's John Bogle. Active stock picking—the kind that gives you the long printout of ever-changing individual positions—is an expensive game. Managers are expensive, research is expensive, commissions are expensive, and taxes are expensive. After all of these are subtracted from your returns, you are better off simply taking a free ride on the back of the stock market by buying an index fund and leaving the active trading to others. To be sure, some managers will beat the market, but few have demonstrated any long-term ability in doing so. For those who do, their success proves their undoing, as they soon are flooded with more hot money from new investors than they know how to invest intelligently. Meanwhile, trying to discover these genius active managers before they beat the market is a study in frustration.

Bogle discovered that the passive index fund buy-and-hold investor generally beats the active investor by a shockingly large margin. Study after study has confirmed the wisdom of holding the whole market, staying invested through thick and thin, and minimizing all frictional costs. While over any one or two years the margin of the advantage may be small or even negative, over a 20-year period your chances of beating the market by picking active managers versus using a low expense, passive, market index fund are only about 15 percent. Over an investment lifetime, this advantage amounts to a fortune. You are taking a lot of money that was going to be transferred from you to the financial services industry and putting it back in your pocket. By switching from active stock picking to a passive portfolio of index funds, you promote yourself from someone who uses a strategy that usually does not work to someone who uses a strategy that consistently does. Anyone who tells you otherwise either has not read the data, or else has a financial stake in your coming to a different conclusion.

This is the paradox: You can spend a few minutes every year managing a passive index portfolio and beat about 85 percent of investors over the long run, or you can devote every minute of your spare time to picking stocks and get a few good hits here and there but end up underperforming the market, as an honest accounting of your performance would reveal. This is not a game worth playing. It is especially not a good use of your time.

It's relatively easy to bring more sanity to your financial life. All you have to do is invest in a few broad market index funds. This way, you take on the risks of the market, and you earn the returns of the market, less the very slight expenses of owning the funds. A U.S. total stock market index fund (ticker: VTI), a total international stock index fund (ticker: VEU), and a total bond market index fund (ticker: BND) cover all your needs. That's all, folks! If someone robs this book from you at gunpoint right now, and that is your only takeaway, you'll be way ahead of the crowd.

Is that all there is? No, there are a few things you can do at the margins to further increase your returns.

Exploiting Market Anomalies for Fun and Profit

Academic researchers Eugene Fama and Ken French studied the long-term returns from stock market investing and concluded that certain strategies have historically delivered greater returns than has the stock market as a whole. For example, *value investors* (investors who buy stocks that sell at a low multiple of their underlying economic value) do better than growth investors. Growth investors buy the stocks that people love, but precisely because these companies are so popular, people tend to overpay for them. This means that in aggregate their long-term returns won't be as good. In comparison, value stock pickers buy companies that are unloved and possibly in some distress, as reflected by their higher book values, higher dividend yields, and earnings that must be used to entice investors. Often they will turn out to be duds, but at least investors didn't overpay. The earnings surprises for value stocks occur more often on the upside. Is this finding valuable? According to Fama/French's data, $1 invested in large U.S. growth stocks in 1926 grew to be worth $1,647 in 2010. One dollar invested in large U.S. value stocks in 1926 grew to be worth $4,599 over the same period.

A second market anomaly is that *small company* stocks tend to do better than large company stocks. Some of them disappear, but others will grow into the next Microsoft. It's impossible to tell which is which, so owning a whole basket of small company stocks is necessary. Does this work? Let's turn to the Fama/French data set once more. One dollar invested in large U.S. companies in 1926 grew to $2,436 in 2010. One dollar invested in small U.S. companies grew to be worth $13,666. You don't need to be a statistician to see that these are meaningful differences.

A third market anomaly is that *low beta* stocks perform better than expected on a risk-adjusted basis. These are stocks that do not respond to movements in the larger stock market with as much volatility as other companies do. We think that the best explanation of this concept comes from John Maynard Keynes, who was a highly successful investor as well as a brilliant economist. Writing in his *General Theory*, Keynes despaired that at the end of the day all our careful calculations about the future earnings of companies can fall apart like a cheap suit. It is very difficult to come up with a reliable value today for a company's future earnings. Compounding this problem is that most people—businessmen and investors alike—are in it for the excitement of speculation and the chance to get rich, which rouses their "animal spirits" and causes them to get too excited about future prospects not exactly in the bank yet.

However, not all companies are equally vulnerable to this exaggeration. There are some companies for which we have a clearer idea of their prospects than we do for others. They have well-established business models and earn money steadily. We can't be 100 percent sure, of course, but we can estimate more reliably the earnings of a Consolidated Edison over the next five years than we can for Google. This means there will be less emotion packaged into the price of Con Ed's stock than there is in Google's, which is more speculative and dependent on future growth projections coming true. Companies like Con Ed are not going to bounce around as much in response to general market events. We might be wrong about this one or that one, but it's unlikely that we would be wrong on average about a basket of such companies. We are less likely to overpay for them, which means that our returns should be better in the long run. The real problem in stock investing comes from overpaying.

A classic low beta stock is Warren Buffett's Berkshire Hathaway. Since Buffett and his sidekick, Charlie Munger, take little active role in running the subsidiaries of this holding company, they look for relatively idiot-proof businesses when making acquisitions. Almost any of the companies they buy could have been in business 100 years ago. Coca-Cola. Candy. Insurance. Trains. The classic low beta stocks are often from the consumer staple, utility, and health care sectors, where there is a constant demand for everyday products that get used up quickly and need to be replaced. Over time, their returns stack up like those of the market as a whole, but with less volatility. It's not that they do so well; it's that more speculative stocks tend to disappoint, as does speculation in general.

But wait! Haven't we just contradicted ourselves? On the one hand, we maintain that markets are extremely efficient and that all available pertinent information is speedily processed into the price of stocks. This supports the whole idea of index-based investing. There is no better estimate of the price of the S&P 500 index than the price it is selling at right now. If individual market participants don't have special insights into the prices of stocks that are superior to those of all investors in the world already distilled into those prices, the least bad way to invest is just to own the whole stock market by using a cheap index fund and be done with it.

However, now we are saying that there are these special factors we can exploit and beat the market. People have known about these market anomalies for years. Why haven't they disappeared? Why doesn't everyone buy value, small, and low beta stocks? The answer seems to be market psychology. Psychology seems to lie behind all the ways that potentially improve stock market returns.

∼

Psychology seems to lie behind all the ways that potentially improve stock market returns.

- Ordinary investors are seriously overconfident of their ability to beat the market, and so they gamble to pick winning stocks. This rarely works. This gives the edge to index funds, which don't bother to pick stocks and just own the whole market, which is less likely to be overpriced (unless the whole market is overpriced).
- Investors love to speculate on glamour companies so they overpay for growth stocks, which lose out over time to "little engine that could" value stocks.
- Investors enjoy the familiarity of owning the big name brand companies everyone has heard of, and that attention raises the market price. They pass on the less familiar, less liquid small stocks that

outperform them over time in aggregate because they are cheaper in the first place.

- Investors eschew boring, old-fashioned businesses that are past their sell date in favor of emotional companies, and so they undervalue low beta stocks.

If true, this is good news, because it means that these effects are not going away anytime soon. There are plenty of stooges like us who are consistently going to fall for the market's head fakes. Since these anomalies seem to be grounded in the foibles of human nature, we should be able to make money off them for a long time to come—or so we hope.

Capture that Anomaly!

Fortunately, there are many mutual funds that let us capture these recognized anomalies (some call them special risk factors). What funds would we use?

Value and Small Company Stocks

Here the world splits into two types of investors: people—often high-net-worth types—who have investment advisors with access to Dimensional Funds (DFA), and people who prefer to do it themselves. We will address both groups.

Dimensional Fund Advisors (DFA) is a mutual fund company started by some professors and others from the University of Chicago, where much of the original work analyzing historical stock market returns was done. DFA subscribes to the passive, market-wide investing model à la Bogle, but believes that returns can be improved by tilting their portfolio to include more small company and value stocks. Their funds are exceedingly well thought out and their returns have been excellent, but you need to go through the intermediary of a financial advisor to access them. DFA regards "hot money" as anathema and uses investment advisors as gatekeepers to make sure they only let in patient, long-term investors. While their expenses are reasonably low, the need for an advisor adds another layer of fees to acquiring their funds.

Advisors who use Dimensional Funds could buy DFA Global Equity Institutional Portfolio (ticker: DGEIX), which wraps up the entire equity investment world into a ball using Dimensional's trademark small company/value tilt. In practice, most advisors will slice and dice this further by region: U.S. Equity, Foreign Developed Markets, Emerging Markets, and so on.

Do-it-yourselfers can capture the small/value premiums by using the fundamental-weighted Powershares FTSE RAFI portfolios: two for the U.S. (tickers: PRF and PRFZ, covering large and small cap stocks), two for foreign developed markets (tickers: PXF and PDN, also covering large and small cap foreign stocks), and one for the emerging markets (ticker: PXH). If you equally weight these five funds in your portfolio you come remarkably close to matching the U.S./Foreign Developed/Emerging Market weights as they exist in the global economy, although most U.S. investors prefer to have most of their stocks in U.S. companies.

Low Beta Stocks

Unfortunately, there is not a single mutual fund specializing in low beta stocks. Therefore, we are going to have to access this effect using low beta stocks and sector funds. Even DFA does not have an offering in this space.

As mentioned previously, our favorite low beta stock is Warren Buffett's Berkshire Hathaway (ticker: BRKB). It is like a mutual fund all by itself, since it is essentially a holding company for many other companies. We could round this out by buying low beta global sector funds: iShares Global Consumer Staples (ticker: KXI), iShares Global Health Care (ticker: IXJ), and iShares Global Utilities (ticker: JXI).

How much should we use in the way of low beta stocks? We have to remember that these will not beat the market when the stock market is racing upwards, but they help limit risk when the market corrects. Let's say our baseline portfolio is 50 percent United States, 40 percent foreign developed markets, and 10 percent emerging markets, all with a small and value company tilt. Reserving 5 to 10 percent of the equity total for low beta stocks should give us slightly higher risk-adjusted returns than a portfolio that was benchmarked to the standard index funds at those weights. If some enterprising mutual fund company would create an inexpensive low beta index fund (hint, hint), we might recommend a higher allocation. Unfortunately, mutual fund companies are in business to make money, and there's nothing sexy to market with a low beta stock fund.

Bonds

This brings us to the 40 part of the 60/40: bonds. The bond market is ruthlessly efficient and there are no special anomalies to exploit here. Bonds are also more democratic, in that retail investors can typically do just as well as institutional investors by buying cheap bond index funds. Bonds expose us to two sources of risk that investors historically have been paid to bear: *term risk* and *credit risk*.

Term risk means that investors who lend money for a long time expect to be paid more than investors who lend money for a short time. That is because over a longer period of time there is a greater risk that interest rates will rise from what they are today, lowering the value of our bond in the process. Consider the plight of an investor in this situation: If the bond he bought pays a 5 percent coupon, but interest rates have risen since he bought it and new bonds today pay 10 percent, his bond simply isn't going to be worth as much as the prices of the two income streams that the bonds represent equilibrate. There is also the risk that inflation will erode the purchasing power of his coupons and the return of principal, making them worth progressively less than the more expensive dollars that he originally lent to the bond issuer. The longer the bond's maturity, the greater the chance that inflation and/or rising interest rates (which often go together) will erode the value of his investment. This means investors usually get paid more in yield the longer the term for which they are lending their money.

Credit risk means that some borrowers are more likely to default on their repayments than others. Investors who take a bigger gamble on getting paid back expect to be paid more than those who lend money to borrowers whose repayment is certain. You are in this situation when you apply for a mortgage. If your credit score is good, you will pay a lower rate of interest than will your deadbeat brother-in-law.

As we go out in years until maturity and down in grades of credit quality, the risks—and potentially the rewards—of our bond investment go up. Interestingly, though, we soon reach a point of diminishing returns along both dimensions. Very long maturity bonds (say, 30 years) are much more volatile than intermediate maturity bonds, while offering only slightly more yield in compensation. High yield ("junk") bonds of low credit quality usually pay little if any more than investment grade bonds after accounting for defaults.

What to Buy

While some people buy bonds to produce a stream of income, many investors use bonds simply to reduce the volatility of their stock portfolios to where they can sleep through the night.

To lower portfolio volatility, we want to use:

- *Short-duration, high quality bonds*: The iShares Barclays 1–3 Year Treasury Bond ETF (ticker: SHY) gets you U.S. Treasuries at 1.9 year's duration for the price of a 0.15 percent expense ratio annually. These work because there is very little default risk, and the short duration limits the interest rate risk. For investors in the higher tax brackets who put bonds in their taxable accounts, short maturity municipal bonds would be considered safe: Vanguard's Short-Term Tax-Exempt Fund (ticker: VWSTX, other share classes available)

give you 1.2 years in duration of AA-rated bonds
for 0.20 percent in annual expenses.

- *Inflation-indexed bonds:* Inflation-indexed bonds have
  even lower correlations to stocks than Treasuries
  do, because in addition to controlling for default
  and maturity risk, they also take out inflation
  risk. Their payout is adjusted according to the
  Consumer Price Index every year. This means
  they provide even better volatility control. iShares
  Barclays TIPs Fund (ticker: TIP) is a good answer
  here, especially for tax-deferred accounts.

- *Total Bond Market Index Fund:* Many 401(k) plans
  have some variant of a total bond market index fund
  among their offerings. This fund takes more credit
  and interest rate risk than the ones above, but all
  things considered it still may be your best choice.
  Since bonds are tax-inefficient, this is a good use
  of your tax-sheltered account, and the bond market
  index fund will usually be one of the least overpriced selections on the menu.

A Risk-Balanced Bond Portfolio

The idea of using bonds as above to put a lid on overall
portfolio volatility works best for someone who is looking
to get his returns from stocks—in other words, someone

using the old-school 60/40. Another way is to use fixed income as a source of return in its own right. To do this, we would expand our bond universe to include four types of bonds and expose ourselves to four risk factors:

1. Maturity risk (Treasury bonds)
2. Credit risk (corporate bonds)
3. Inflation risk (inflation-indexed bonds)
4. Currency risk (unhedged foreign sovereign bonds)

Phil has designed a bond portfolio that tries to spread its risks evenly among these. It looks like Figure 2.1. It is not the final word on the subject, but it's a start.

This portfolio is still short in maturity and high in credit quality, but it is more diversified and has higher projected returns and risks than the all-short-term bonds

Figure 2.1   A Risk-Balanced Bond Portfolio

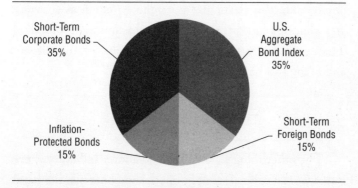

Short-Term Corporate Bonds 35%

U.S. Aggregate Bond Index 35%

Inflation-Protected Bonds 15%

Short-Term Foreign Bonds 15%

approach above. We are exposing ourselves to more risks on the bond side, either just because we feel like it, or possibly because we intend to create a portfolio with more bond-centered risks and less equity risk. This is still a relatively low dose of risk, but with the bond market in the state it is in today, we wouldn't recommend taking on more unless you are personally a bond vigilante. Using the bond portfolio above we estimate that we could change overall allocation from 60/40 stocks/bonds to 55/45 and be at the same place with our risks and returns, just by spreading our risks around a little bit more.

All Together Now

All these various asset classes are the building blocks of a more efficient stock-and-bond portfolio, 60/40 or otherwise. Figure 2.2 shows how they might fit together in a souped-up portfolio—cranked to 55/45. We are not recommending this particular portfolio so much as showing you what one interpretation of this dream might look like. There are many possible interpretations of this dream and many will be better than this one.

Luck is a terrible strategy.

The other thing to keep in mind always and everywhere is that we can control strategy but the outcome is in the hand

Figure 2.2   A Better 60/40?

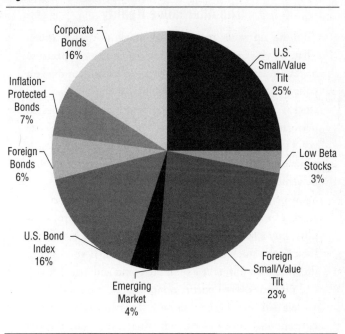

of the gods. You can spend all your money on lottery tickets and if you win the Super Powerball lottery you will become rich overnight. That doesn't mean buying lottery tickets with your money was a smart strategy or that you are some kind of genius—it simply means you were lucky. Luck, however, is a terrible strategy. Over time, we hope that having a good strategy will converge with a fortunate outcome but, cruelly, there are no guarantees.

The Alternative Reality

To tune up your conventional stock portfolio, dump whatever you are doing and invest in a few broad-spectrum market index funds. If you want to do more than this, tilt your portfolio toward value, small company, and low beta stocks. In doing so, you improve your long-term expected performance, but be aware that you will also experience years when you will underperform the benchmark indices while on the road to Shangri-La. In the future, there may be vehicles to exploit other market anomalies as well.

When it comes to the bond side of your portfolio, you reach a fork in the road. If you just want to control volatility, buy all short-term or inflation-protected bonds and look to the stock market for your returns. If you want to do more than this, take a bit more credit and maturity risk and tilt your overall portfolio more to the bond side.

We will circle back to the overall portfolio allocation—conventional investments plus alternatives—in the last chapter of this book.

Chapter Three

Collectibles as Investments

---- ∿ ----

Beauty in the Eye of the Marketplace

PERHAPS YOU EXPECT THAT YOUR AUTHORS will be uncritical cheerleaders for alternative investments. Far from it. We're going to prove that by getting tough on some categories of alternatives that we think you should avoid. The first one of these is collectibles.

During times of economic dislocation—when people lose faith in conventional instruments like stocks, and bonds—investment dollars are often allocated to various unconventional vehicles. A mysterious and fervent devotion attaches itself to rare collectible items like watches, art, coins, stamps, books, jewels, antiques, wine, rugs, horses, paintings, carpets, sports memorabilia, automobiles, and various similar exotica. This can happen in good times, too.

Throughout history, people have sought to hedge themselves against national financial disaster by carrying off and hoarding beautiful relics. In his *Decline and Fall of the Roman Empire* (or was it the movie *Gladiator*, we don't remember), Edward Gibbon notes that when pitiful Romans fled their cities under the barbarian onslaught, they took with them statuary, mosaics, and tapestries in the hope that they could be exchanged for far more than the thoroughly debased Roman currency. Similar things happened in the South during the American Civil War, and after the World War II in Europe, as the defeated countries found that their currencies were worthless.

Love and Pleasure

Devoted students and collectors in many different fields have discovered that they can turn their love affairs with various tangible items into cash. Men and women who have dedicated their lives to learning the most minute details of recondite fields occasionally can find that their skill and time have given them valuable assets. That said, the basic story on collectibles is this: Collect for love, not for money.

~

**The basic story on collectibles is this:
Collect for love, not for money.**

There are enormous drawbacks to collecting as a financial endeavor. As P. T. Barnum said, there is a sucker born every minute and two to take him. The country is crawling with fast-buck Freddies trying to convince the many suckers of our age that collecting is easy, fun, and profitable.

So, here are a few rules from one sucker to another.

Rule One: If it is advertised in a mass-circulation journal as rare and important and potentially valuable, stay away, unless you like it for its own sake.

Items that specifically are made to be collectible almost never are. That special commemorative medal struck by Acme Tool & Die we bought to commemorate the inauguration of Vice-President Joe Biden? Turns out, it's not that valuable—even though it was advertised in *TV Guide*. Things like this have no intrinsic value except to make money for the manufacturer. There is rarely a secondary market because they were not that rare, precious, or beautiful in the first place.

Rule Two: Collecting goes in fads.

Around the turn of the twentieth century there were crazes for collecting medieval manuscripts. J.P. Morgan and other tycoons collected illuminated manuscripts and other exotic books from all over the world. Staggering prices were paid for them until the early 1920s. Then the fad abruptly disappeared. Today, those manuscripts will barely fetch the prices they reached 85 years ago. The same has been true of Italian marble statuary. Much beloved in the Roaring Twenties and into the 1930s, it has never returned even what it was selling for during the Great Depression. All those medieval manuscripts in your study and marble statues in your garden? They probably aren't worth as much as you thought. Sorry.

Because collectibles generally have little intrinsic value, only people's wishes make them come true. When the fashion passes, the collector is left with a drawer full of old PEZ dispensers or whatever seemed so desirable at the time. In that sense, collectibles are like chain letters. As long as the chain keeps going, everyone is fine. But when the chain stops, the last person who paid out the money is in trouble. Beware of fads unless you are deeply in love with the faddish item and do not care what other people think about it or about making money on it.

Rule Three: Beware of thinly traded markets.

The market for collectibles can be about as liquid as the market for stolen Vermeers. To find oneself at an art auction, whipped into a frenzy of enthusiasm and confidence that a certain item will make you rich and happy, is one thing. The auctioneer will cheerfully accept your money and congratulate you as he hands over the painting and moves on to the next item on the block.

To try to get your money out at the other end is a horse of a different color. When the time comes to sell, you will have to essay the haphazard methods traditionally associated with selling a used car.

Rule Four: If you cannot afford to be patient, either financially or temperamentally, find another hobby.

Collectibles can be subject to wild swings in value even when they are in constant demand. They do not diversify the rest of your investments, because their prices are highest precisely when stock markets are bubbling. Then, since collectibles are the epitome of discretionary expenditures, they are the first to be dispensed with during hard times. As "high beta" objects whose price swings amplify market moves, they should be held in the smallest of quantities, if at all, and by people who will never have to sell them to raise money. Therefore, our basic guidance on collectibles is to discourage collecting for purely speculative reasons. Yes, lovers of beauty and lifetime aficionados of even the most esoteric items do stand to make money. In the world of Louis XVI clock collectors, there are profits to be made by the Louis XVI clock collector who knows what time it is. However, the true collector will derive immense psychic pleasure—the most important kind—whether his object pays off in cash or not.

Buying and Selling

Our delight in all things collectible is going to be sullied by having to buy and sell said items. When it comes to buying a collectible, you will always pay retail. Even if you are told that you are not paying retail, you still will be paying retail, and that is a lot more than wholesale. In other words, you will be buying high and selling low. If you must insist on collecting with any thought of financial return, try to inform yourself how you will dispose of your bijou once the time comes. Never rely on what the smiling salesperson tells you as he rings the cash register. If it were so valuable, with such effortless profit potential, why would he sell it to you?

When the time does come to sell, you can try advertisements in the appropriate journals or consignment to auctioneers. You can sell it directly to a dealer. You can list it on eBay or on some specialized auction site devoted to your hobby. In any case, be prepared for a shock. Unless you as a collector are also proprietor of a gallery, you can completely forget about getting the retail price of your bauble. Even though art magazines or friends tell you your collectible has increased in value, this will not prove to be the case when you try to sell it. You will find the private auctioneer takes a generous cut of whatever your objet d'art fetches. Moreover, even the best, most prestigious auctioneers will not always be able to sell your beloved item at once.

Exception: If you can get yourself elected trustee of a museum—a select bunch of bananas, to be sure—you can use the position to lobby for exhibitions for whoever the flavor-of-the-month is that you and your curators have been collecting lately. Don't forget to hire an art history Ph.D. student to write some mumbo-jumbo for the catalog—that will really add class. Then you and your pals can liquidate your holdings at a tidy profit.

We fear that PBS's *Antiques Roadshow* gives viewers a misleading impression of the easy money to be made trafficking in collectibles. Their appraisers always tell people the *insurance* value or the *replacement* value of the gewgaw they have hauled in, or what it might fetch in some ideal auction before expenses (for some reason, it's always $5,000). What they don't say is what they, the knowledgeable dealer, would pay for it in cash money right there and then on the spot, or what we might call the *actual value*. That would be the revelation.

It's always fun to watch the delight on the face of somebody who paid $250 for a painting in 1950 when he discovers that it's supposedly worth $5,000 today. What this scenario doesn't show is the opportunity cost: If he'd just put that same $250 in the stock market in 1950, he'd have $130,000 today. Then again, maybe he extracted $125,000 worth of enjoyment from having it sit in his attic. Pride of ownership can be difficult to quantify.

eBay has created its own set of perturbations to the collectibles market. Initially, the net effect was to drive down the price of many items, as people discovered that there were more first editions of *Slaughterhouse Five* around than they were led to believe by ye olde rare book dealer with the one moldy copy on his shelf. However, bringing more liquidity to what was once an entirely dealer-rigged market, and inserting more anonymity and distance into the process, has also exacerbated preexisting conditions, such as fraud. Is that Rolex real, or is it a fake? What about that Ernie Banks baseball card? Or that 1957 Gibson Les Paul guitar? Is it even possible any longer to tell an expert reproduction from an original? If it is, and if you can't, how are you going to find the someone who can? The field is full of unscrupulous operators and charlatans at every level; if Sotheby's and Christie's can conspire to fix prices (the "tone at the top"), look out below.

All these perils will become clearer if we take one collectible as a case study. Let's take classic cars.

How Not to Make Money

Wouldn't it be cool to drive a red 1957 gull-wing Mercedes 300SL? Girls would be checking you out up and down the strip, plus it would be a blast to drive, plus it would go up in value year after year. It would be like getting paid to have fun and be popular. It would even subsidize your transportation budget.

That's the dream. The reality is different.

The only correct way to assess the prices of cars would be to measure the price set by the forces of supply and demand. In other words, people who sold their cars at auction without a reserve price (a price below which they will not sell but instead take their buggy and go home) would get a true gauge of prices. However, almost no cars are sold at auction without reserve prices being set for them. The most foolish seller is not so foolish as to offer to sell without requiring that a certain price be reached. At many exotic car auctions more than half of the cars do not fetch their reserve.

Second, a prevalent way of "establishing" the price of a collector's car is fraught with deceit. Most collectible cars are exchanged through private sales, either between individuals or with a dealer acting on one side as principal or agent. Accurate price information on the cars in these trades is impossible to obtain. Collectors are usually close-mouthed about the price of a car, wishing to hide either embarrassment or taxable income. Dealers naturally want to conceal costs as well as their own profits.

Many of these trades involve groups of exotic cars. Suppose three fairly exotic cars are exchanged for one very exotic car. Then the parties to the trade, if they are in a publicity-seeking mood, may tell an auto magazine that their cars sold for $300,000 for the most exotic car and an average of $100,000 per for the rather less exotic cars. But who knows if those are the true prices? The parties can assign the price arbitrarily.

Another pitfall for unwary buyers is the failure to distinguish between real price and nominal price. The real price is the price adjusted for inflation. Porsches in good condition dating from the 1960s sell for far more today than what they cost when new, which sounds good until we realize that a loaf of bread today sells for more than seven times more than one did in the 1960s. So does almost everything else, on average. Taking the price of an item in dollars unadjusted for inflation is meaningless. Even if you are buying a car that is an exception to this rule (which is to say you are paying an exceptionally high price for the car), you have to hope that the price keeps on being exceptional. That outcome is not inevitable. The price could also regress to the mean as some other type of car suddenly becomes more fashionable than yours.

Oh, and did we mention that you have to restore the car? A typical restoration job takes about 800 hours and a couple of years at a custom garage. You know how you always wonder if Sven is ripping you off when he fixes your wife's Volvo? Add another zero. These guys are going to become like family, but not necessarily in a good way. Those vintage, original equipment manufacturer parts you need? You will need a second mortgage to afford them.

One more thing: Classic cars were designed before the aid of computers. Their handling compares to a wheelbarrow. A Honda Civic will smoke them through the twists and turns. They don't work well, the radios are horrible, the heaters, ditto, electrical, ditto, forget about A/C, and as far as safety equipment goes, you're lucky if they have seat belts. We once complained about the radio in an old car. The dealer informed us, "You have to understand—Mercedes thinks of the radio as a way to communicate troop movements." There's a good reason why they don't make them anymore. The design is unmatched, but that is all.

It is not easy to convert money into beauty and then back into money again.

In summary, no one without a generation's experience in dealing with exotic cars should expect to escape disaster collecting cars for profit. But if the investor loves his car and derives great satisfaction from riding in it and watching the envious stares, if he does not begrudge the months his car will spend in the clutches of mechanics and body molders, then he will be all right no matter what. It makes sense for someone like Jay Leno to collect cars. It makes less sense for most of the rest of us.

The Alternative Reality

Here is the takeaway you can stitch into an antique sampler: It is not easy to convert money into beauty and then back into money again. As a songwriter once wrote (in another context), if you're gonna do it, do it for love.

If you decide to indulge anyway, remember that buying and selling collectibles will exaggerate trends already in evidence in the rest of the economy. When the stock market is hot, modern artists will fetch record prices. When we're in a recession, prices of collectibles will be the first to fall. They don't diversify the rest of your holdings or hedge anything.

Lest you think we are singling out collectibles, there are plenty of other alternative investments we aren't going to be recommending anytime soon, as you will see in the next chapter.

Chapter Four

More Alternatives We Don't Love

The Elephant's Graveyard of Financial Products

As Groucho Marx sings in *Horsefeathers*, "Whatever it is, I'm against it!" Well, we're not against everything. Just private equity, buy/write funds, structured products, 130/30 funds, and precious metals. These all have their place, but that place is not in your portfolio. Here's why . . .

Private Equity

Private equity is often mentioned in the same breath as hedge funds as the preferred investment for the elite. What is private equity, anyway? Is there some way the little guy can scoop his bread into this gravy?

Private equity falls into two broad categories: *venture capital* and *leveraged buyouts*. They are alike in that they are both illiquid investments that will tie up your money for years. We will take them on one at a time.

Venture capital is what most people mean by private equity. After a start-up business reaches the point where the hapless founder can no longer run it on his personal credit cards, he needs outside sources of capital to help take his company to the next level. The founder has already tapped out his in-laws, friends, and everybody he knows. He goes to a banker for a loan, but all the banker can see is big dreams, a big stack of debts, and no revenue. What is this entrepreneur to do?

Rich people, pension plans, and endowments are happy to lend him money if they think his fundamental business plan is sound. These folks pool their money into a *venture capital fund,* where the money is allocated by professional managers. The business founder gets the cash he needs like oxygen to stay alive, while the fund gets a piece of the business and a big say in how it is run.

The shareholders of the fund, who coughed up the dough, hit the jackpot when the company is finally taken public. Note that it may take years before there is any return on their investment in the fund, and indeed if the idea doesn't pan out (an ever-present possibility), it may be a total write-off. In the meantime, for the years while they are waiting for all this to come true, there is no market whatsoever for the business or any piece of the business. The ideal ending is that the company turns into Apple Computer, and in fact most venture capital funding does go to technology or biotechnology companies. Sounds good, right? Who wouldn't want a bite of the next Apple?

Investors willing to tie up their money for years in ultra-small companies require compensation for bearing these risks. If brilliant portfolio managers like Yale's David Swensen are willing to sink 17 percent of their money into this asset class, shouldn't you?

Almost certainly not.

Why not?

Let us count the ways.

In the first place, the big returns accruing to private equity in general are averages. Some stocks will become the next Google while many others go into the landfill. However, the average venture capital investor will not get that average of these returns. He will get some particular return. A lucky one will get Apple and 99 will draw blanks. In other words, the field is strewn with land mines. Do you feel lucky (punk)? Do you?

What the actual returns are from venture capital investing is a mystery wrapped in a taco. Why? The funds are under no obligation to report their returns to anyone except their shareholders. Driessem, Lin, and Phalippou, writing for the National Bureau of Economic Research, tried to figure out what these returns were and concluded that venture capital has negative alpha coupled with a very high beta. Translation: It underperforms the stock market while amplifying the stock market's risks.

What does this mean to us as investors? This is exactly the opposite profile from what we want. Remember how we argued earlier that most people need to reduce the stock market exposure in their lives? Private equity is like public equity on steroids. It exaggerates market returns. These tiny companies carry market risk that cannot be diversified away.

Parenthetically, this means that if you are a private equity investor, the rest of your portfolio should look as little like the equity market as possible. Venture capitalists fall prey to the psychological fallacy of investing by story. Because they love the story behind the business, they overestimate the potential returns and underestimate the real risks. In other words, they are human beings.

The other type of private equity is a *leveraged buyout fund*. Here the investors have a public company in their sights that they think they can run better than its present management is doing. Strange to say, there seem to be a large number of corporations whose stock is so wildly underpriced that private equity can step in, buy them at above-market prices, and still make money by spiffing them up.

While this would seem to violate efficient market theory, other explanations are possible.

An alternative reading is that these deals are often done in cahoots with the management of the acquired company, who know exactly how to change the company and make it worth more, but will only put that knowledge to work if they can reap the rewards from the repair job themselves instead of giving it all to the shareholders.

Another explanation is that the buyout fund has acquired a public company, done some accounting tricks with reserves and allowances to make it appear profitable, and plans to resell it to the public for a big profit. Accounting is, after all, more art than science at the highest levels.

Then there is the old "rip, strip, and flip": The fund buys the company and has it issue junk bonds. The company gets saddled with debt from these high-interest instruments, while the fund managers pay themselves immense dividends and fees from the proceeds of the bond sale. This lets them cash out with a profit before they even start to reorganize the now-hobbled company, whose subsequent performance is now less transparent and a matter of relative indifference, at least to them. Back in the 1980s Drexel Burnham Lambert facilitated a chain of these transactions until their junk bonds massively defaulted.

Leveraged buyouts claim to align the interests of shareholders and managers, but levering the company to the max simply creates the familiar "heads I win, tails you lose" scenario for the fund managers and creates a far more glaring conflict of interest than would ever have occurred had the company remained public. Other people disagree, however, and feel that this kind of activity contributes economic value to society. You make the call.

How to Make Money in Private Equity

The best way to get into private equity is to run your own fund and invest other people's money. The compensation befits a Maharaja. First, you get a 2 percent management fee every year just for turning on the lights. Then you get 20 percent of any profits. Finally, you can charge additional deal fees and fees for "monitoring" the fund's investments.

As for David Swensen and his ilk, are they crazy? Not a bit. They have access to the finest talent pool money can buy. They get in first on all the prime deals, while everyone else gets leftovers. There is too much money chasing the rest of the deals for them to be profitable to anyone except the fund managers.

That said, we do have one private equity idea we like: Berkshire Hathaway (ticker: BRKB). It is run by Warren Buffett, the most successful capital allocator in history, and he manages his $200 billion company for a salary of $100,000 a year. As a private equity play, Berkshire is diluted by large holdings in public companies. Buffett keeps his eye on every nickel, so he will tend to underbid private equity funds in making new acquisitions. Then again, Berkshire has a money bin that enables it to do deals (like their acquisition of the Burlington Northern Santa Fe railroad) of a scope that no one else could touch.

~

**One private equity idea we like:
Warren Buffett's Berkshire Hathaway.**

Some people recommend buying Goldman Sachs (ticker: GS) as a private equity play, since Goldman seems to be collecting a toll at the crossroads of every deal. However, we question how much of that benefit actually flows to shareholders. Most of it seems to go to the partners and never is seen again.

You can also buy mutual funds that invest in companies that own private equity funds such as KKR (ticker: KKR) but why would you want to, since they would presumably concentrate your total risk in the rest of your portfolio instead of diversifying it?

"Buy/Write" Funds

Before we explain why we aren't fans of these alternative funds, we are going to have to explain what they are. They start when a manager buys a stock index (such as the S&P 500) and then sells *covered calls* against it. What are covered calls, you ask? These are transactions where, in exchange for some cash, a buyer of a covered call option is given the right (or "option") to "call away" the underlying stock from its present owner, if the stock price rises to a certain level by a certain date. If the stock index falls, stays the same, or doesn't rise far enough, the money paid for the expired call option amounts to an extra bonus to the stock owner. If the market goes up a lot, then the stock owner gets the gains up to the strike price of the call option, but the gains thereafter go to the buyer of the covered call option, who becomes the new owner of the stock at that strike price and calls it away. The seller of the call option would rather keep the stock in that situation, of course, but that is the gamble he took.

The income from the call options is not a free good. Notice that this strategy delivers nearly all the downside of equities with the upside clipped off. That does not ordinarily strike us as a good deal (depending on the price).

Some funds take this a step further. They take the money from selling the covered calls and use it to buy out-of-the-money *puts* on the underlying index. This means if the market falls, they can "put" it to somebody else, effectively limiting their downside exposure. They are exposed to the downside to a certain price, but thereafter they have bought the right (or "option") to stick it to somebody else.

Selling calls and buying puts places a collar around the portfolio and gives you a stock index fund that will move within the channel created by the puts and calls—neither going up nor falling as far as the stock market in the extreme cases.

Why aren't we fans? Because you can get the same risk/return profile more cheaply simply by not investing as much in equities in the first place. We were able to simulate the total returns of a buy/write fund from 1994 to 2010 almost to the penny just by putting half our money in the S&P 500 index fund and keeping the rest in T-bills. In other words, if you want to control risk, you don't have to pay fund managers extra money to do it for you this way. You can accomplish the same thing just by keeping half your money in the bank and taking your lumps in the stock market with the rest.

Structured Products

Structured products are products that are carefully structured to make money for the people who sell them, at the expense of the unfortunate individuals who buy them. They were created to take advantage of people's gambling instincts and poor mathematical understanding of the trade-offs associated with investing in the options market. Like a bar bet, these odds often can be presented in attractive terms, such as, "We're offering you all the upside of the emerging markets index with only a fraction of the downside risk!" One thing you can bank on: The creators of these products have done the math, and they have no intention to lose money on the transaction themselves. If you have a brokerage account serviced by commissioned salespeople, it is very likely that they have tried to sell you some of these, and unless you bravely resisted their arm-twisting, you already own some.

The structured products themselves are issued by investment banks and typically consist of two parts: a *note* and a *derivative*. A note is an IOU. The derivative adjusts the terms of the final payoff according to the performance of some other asset from which it derives its value (hence, *derivative*).

Would an example help? You buy an IOU that, upon coming due, promises to pay you either a portion of the returns of the S&P 500 Index over the loan period on the upside, or, at worst, simply gives you all your money back if the market doesn't go up. How would this work?

A simplified example: The bank takes your money and buys a bond that matures on the same date your note does. You give the bank $1,000 and they buy a bond for $900. This gives them $100 to play with.

They keep a portion for themselves and, with the remaining money, they buy an option on the S&P 500 Index at today's price that will come due on the same date the note matures. If the S&P 500 Index falls between now and then, the option expires worthless, and the bank hands you your money back. If the option is in the money, they take the payout and divide it with you.

There are innumerable variations on this theme. These derivatives can be linked to anything: stock indexes, convertible bonds, an individual stock, foreign currencies, or your Uncle Charley's cholesterol level—anything people might be motivated to gamble upon. Usually, though, it's dressed up to sound like a risk-free investment, or at least one where the upside is comically greater than the downside.

What's not to love?

First of all, these investments are illiquid. There is no market for them. With most structured products, you bought it, you own it, and you will have to hold it to maturity.

Then, what exactly do you own? Despite all the talk about the possible fat returns from the index or stock to which it is linked, you basically own an unsecured IOU from the company that sold it to you. What if the company goes bankrupt? In that case, you own a piece of paper. Get in line to try and collect. This is precisely what happened to the people who bought structured products from Lehman Brothers, the distinguished 158-year-old firm that was one of the leading sellers of these notes (with a 10 percent market share) until it went bankrupt in 2008.

Because so many people lost huge amounts of money on structured products during the credit crisis, the indefatigable helpers of Wall Street have created a new version that has FDIC insurance. These are more expensive, because part of your money is going to buy the insurance policy. They are peddled as "CDs," but the term here is only a sales metaphor. When you buy a real CD, if your uncle lands in jail and you need to bail him out, you can break open the piggy bank if you are willing to take a haircut on the interest. With the structured note "CD," you can check in but you can't check out.

Another benefit (to the broker) is that—because there is no market for these securities once sold—they can be carried at a made-up price on your account statement.

These instruments are very difficult to understand and you need a computer to analyze them. This gives the issuer a chance to bury their fees deep within a web of mystery, which means they have the dream combination of being expensive and yet having invisible fees.

Yet, perversely, structured products are most often marketed as a sure thing to safety-minded investors—the very people who should be the most concerned about the liquidity, credit quality, expense, transparency, risk, and value of their holdings.

Somewhere there is an individual for whom a particular structured product is exactly the thing that would perfectly complement his portfolio. This person has a Ph.D. and is a student of options theory. Does that sound like you?

130/30 Funds

130/30 funds are becoming very popular for some reason. We have nothing against them per se (well, maybe we have a little against them), except that they are proposed as alternative investments. That they assuredly are not.

A 130/30 fund is two funds in one. The manager takes $100 of your money and buys a portfolio of stocks. Then he borrows an additional $60 against it and uses this money to run a market-neutral fund—more on this coming up—which by definition is half long and half short. If you add up the dollars, he has invested $130 long ($100 plus one-half of the $60 he borrowed) and used $30 to short the market, using the other half of the $60 he borrowed to bet that some stocks will go down instead of up.

Add it up and you get 100 percent net market exposure: $130 long minus $30 short equals $100 net long. *For this reason, a 130/30 fund doesn't hedge anything, and consequently, it is not a hedge fund at all.* It should have a correlation to the stock market and a beta of close to one. The great hope here is that it will deliver alpha or extra returns.

Have we mentioned that we are not great believers in alpha stock picking among members of the human race whose last name is not Buffett? Therefore, we were heartened to learn that someone has cooked up a 130/30 index fund. Proshares Credit Suisse 130/30 ETF (ticker: CSM, 0.95 percent expense ratio) ranks stocks along 10 dimensions of value and then buys 130 percent of the ones that look most undervalued and shorts the 30 percent that appear most overvalued. If an investor were determined to go the 130/30 route, this would be a vehicle to look at, at least based on the most casual possible survey of a crowded field. We emphasize that this would be classified as part of the equity portion of the portfolio, not as an alternative investment or portfolio diversifier.

Gold

If you are a king or a pirate, you should have a chest full of gold. If your name is Auric Goldfinger, you will want a Rolls Royce made of gold, because you love only gold. In other cases, however, the need is less compelling.

~

If you are a king or a pirate, you should have a chest full of gold. In other cases, the need is less compelling.

Many people are captivated by gold, especially those who subscribe to a survivalist mentality. If you truly believe that the days of western civilization are numbered and mobs will soon be roaming the streets, a gold coin may be your means to a loaf of bread or your passport to a new life in an exotic locale. That is the subject for another, very depressing book.

Your authors have no great fascination with gold (although we both own tiny amounts). As gold is included in all the commodity index funds we will eventually recommend, we don't see the need for a special allocation.

Like other commodities, gold *should* provide a hedge against inflation, provide a store of value as paper currencies become increasingly worthless, hedge against political risk, and be generally uncorrelated with the stock and bond markets. It has served some and all of these roles at various points in the past, but there are no guarantees that it will serve any and all of these roles in the future.

Whether or not there is a modern portfolio theory case for gold as a separate asset class depends entirely on the start and stop dates we choose to make the argument. During certain date ranges, picked after the fact, gold adds a Midas touch. During others—and especially over the long haul—it sits there like lead. The fact that it has gone up a lot recently does not mean that it is going to continue going up even more. There are supposedly special reasons to own gold now (as in, the value of fiat currencies tends to depreciate), but then people have always made up special reasons to own gold. We are concerned that most people will buy exactly when the mystical premium is highest. The subsequent history of commodities that have had a spectacular run up is not a happy story.

Warren Buffett recently put it to your authors this way: You have a choice. On the one hand, you can have all the gold in the world. It fits into a cube of metal about the size of a large McMansion. Or, you can have all the farm land in the United States. Plus, you can own 10 Exxon Mobils. Plus, you can have one trillion dollars of walking-around money. Which would you choose? Which is likely to be the more productive long-term investment?

If You Must Obey the Golden Rule

If you must buy gold as a stand-alone investment, the SPDR Gold Trust ETF (ticker: GLD, expense ratio

0.40 percent) is probably the way to go. GLD takes your money and buys gold bars, keeping them in a giant underground vault in London. No doubt suspecting us to be bank robbers, they wouldn't say exactly where. Some people don't believe the gold is really in the vault, but gullible fools that we are, we believe the audited accounting posted on the www.spdrgoldshares.com website.

We like a little gold just fine in a basket with a lot of other commodities, but have no great interest in it by itself. We always prefer the broader index, to which we turn in the next chapter.

The Alternative Reality

There are plenty of worthwhile alternative investments out there. Unless your situation is extremely unusual, so unusual in fact that we have difficulty offhand imagining what it might be, it is unlikely that private equity, covered call funds, structured products, 130/30 funds, or gold need to have a big place in your life. When in doubt, include it out.

Chapter Five

Conventional Alternatives I: Commodities

~

To Make a Killing, Take Out a Contract

ON THE GREAT HUNT FOR ALTERNATIVE ASSETS TO STOCKS and bonds, our first stop must be commodities. Many of us were introduced to the wonders of commodities as they were explained to Eddie Murphy in the movie *Trading Places*: *coffee . . . that you had for breakfast . . . bacon . . .*

which you might find in a bacon, lettuce, and tomato sandwich.
For our purposes, we expand this list to include:

Agriculture

- Butter
- Cocoa
- Coffee
- Corn
- Cotton
- Lumber
- Milk
- Oats
- Orange Juice
- Rough Rice
- Soybean Meal
- Soybean Oil
- Soybeans
- Sugar
- Wheat
- Wheat (Chicago Wheat)
- Wheat (Kansas Wheat)

Livestock

- Pork Bellies
- Lean Hogs
- Live Cattle
- Feeder Cattle

Energy

- Coal
- Electricity
- Heating Oil
- Gasoil
- Unleaded Regular Gasoline
- Crude Oil
- Brent Crude Oil
- Propane
- Natural Gas

Industrial Metals

- Aluminum
- Copper
- Lead

- Nickel
- Zinc
- Tin

Precious Metal

- Gold
- Silver

- Platinum
- Palladium

However, our friend Jim Rogers recommends, "If you cannot spell commodities, I wouldn't suggest buying commodities." Don't use the above as a shopping list next time you pull your big rig up to Costco. We're talking about buying commodities in something called the *futures market*.

~

As Jim Rogers recommends, "If you cannot spell commodities, I wouldn't suggest buying commodities."

What is the futures market? We're glad you asked.

Back to the Futures Market

Today, the center of the commodities world is the CME Group in Chicago, but the futures market for commodities goes back to Japan in the late seventeenth and early eighteenth centuries. This would have made a great Kurosawa film—*Wall Street, Japanese-style*.

Cut to: Osaka, Japan. Time: the early 1700s. Farmers bring their rice to the Dojima Rice Exchange to sell. A farmer pulls up to a warehouse with a cart full of rice and has to negotiate a price on the spot. The problem was—and is—that rice is harvested only once per year, but people need to eat all year long, so everything was riding on that one big sale. What's a farmer to do?

The rice farmers realized that they needed to find a way to insure against getting a bad price. Otherwise, one bad day could wipe them out (and here we mean, literally, wipe them out). As a result, a way of transacting business was developed that served both parties better. The buyers were willing to guarantee the farmers a price in advance. They would offer them less than the probable final market price, but much more than a possibly disastrous market price. The buyers, on the other side, would be protected from having to pay an exorbitant price if supplies were low. The contract they drew up specified that a set quantity and quality of rice would be delivered at a specified future date to a specified location for this prearranged price.

With all the salient features of the transaction nailed down, a funny thing happened. This *futures contract* itself became a marketable commodity. A futures market—a clearinghouse for all these contracts—arose. This was incredibly useful, because it let everyone know the standard price and meant that individuals on either side of the transaction wouldn't get an unfair (nonstandard) deal. It was beautiful. It got rid of all of the idiosyncratic and counterparty risk of one-off transactions. Over time, this model was applied to all the commodities on our shopping list.

Today, most people trading futures have no intention of either delivering or taking delivery of the underlying commodity. Those stories about the guy who forgot to sell his contract and had a truckload of hogs delivered to his front yard in Scarsdale are apocryphal. However, you don't grow rice. You don't grow cattle. What does this have to do with you and your investments?

How Do Investors Use Futures Markets?

Before we can talk about how to use the futures markets, we need to take a look at the colorful gang of customers who hang out there, at the Chicago Mercantile Exchange— the CME—where everybody knows your name. One group of people are speculators: people who feel they have a better slant on how the price of a certain commodity will shake down than everyone else does. In the movie *Trading Places*, the Duke brothers are in this position. They have illegally obtained an advance copy of the Department of Agriculture's orange juice report and use this information to front-run the market. In your case, you might have a gut feeling about what the price of oil is going to do over the next year, and you might be right. Just be aware that you are trading against Ph.D. energy analysts from Exxon Mobil and Arab sheiks, and it is possible that they know even more about the subject than you do.

Other people you will meet at the exchange are often in some related business and looking to use the futures market to hedge their price. One might be an artisanal coffee grower who grows some fancy type of coffee. There is no specific futures market for coffee like his, so instead he sells contracts for coffee of the standard grade that is the one actually traded. He has no intention of delivering, so he will buy back the contract and cancel it before it comes due. In this way he will "cross hedge" his price with a commodity whose price closely parallels his own. If the price of coffee rises in the meantime, he will pay more when he goes to buy the contract back, but he will also make more money when he sells his own stash. If the price of coffee has fallen, he will not make as much when he sells his private brew, but will make money when he buys the contract back for less than he paid for it. Once again, he has locked in a price, just indirectly. (Yale economist Robert Shiller reports that when he visited the floor of the exchange where coffee futures are traded, he had the nerve to ask for a cup of coffee. They didn't have any.)

A third group at the CME would be people whose businesses depend in some way on the price of the commodity. The Orange Julius company might want to lock in the price of the major ingredient in their devilishly good drink. They don't want summer to arrive and then find their expenses going through the roof because of a poor orange crop earlier that year. It's not easy for them to suddenly raise prices. They can cope by using futures contracts to hedge the price of orange juice months ahead of time. That way, there are no surprises.

So What?

We know what you're thinking. Thanks for the history lesson, but why should commodities be part of my alternative portfolio? To be blunt, commodities are not what economists call *earning* assets—that is, assets that by themselves make money. If you own a plot of land, you can rent it or farm it and produce income. If you own a business, you can make gizmos and sell them at a profit. But if you own a bar of zinc, all it does is sit there. You can look at it, it can look at you, but it doesn't actually do anything to make money for you. The only way it makes money is if somebody wants to pay you more for it than you paid when you bought it.

We can grant that the prices of commodities should keep up with inflation. Because commodities are the basic inputs to everything else, their prices cannot be insulated from a general increase in prices. They are generic—a pound of sugar is the same all over town—so there is no explaining away the uniqueness of a price rise across commodities the way there might be with some manufactured product. If a car or a suit has a price increase, there can always be a special explanation. But prices of commodities are completely elastic and react instantly to market forces.

If all commodity prices did was rise and fall with inflation, owning commodities would be about as enticing as kissing your aunt (of course, that could be very exciting, depending on your aunt). Is there any other reason why commodities should be considered an asset class for investors? Especially if we also concede that few of us are likely to have insights into individual commodity prices that are superior to those of all committed market participants like farmers and miners and oil producers?

The general answer must be supply and demand. To rationalize purchasing commodities, we have to subscribe to the view that demand will keep the prices of commodities rising.

The most popular version of this view may be put thus: As global capitalism transforms much of the world from subsistence agriculture to a post-industrial society with a chicken in every pot and a Starbucks on every street corner, there will be a tremendous demand for commodities for the big build-out.

More briefly still, there is China.

All the new cities being built in Asia are not going to be built out of bamboo. This transformation, if it is going to happen at all, will require *beaucoup de* commodities.

Each commodity has its own supply and demand characteristics. Oil has a library all to itself. Some commodities may be scarcer, some more plentiful, some easier to ramp up production and some harder, and some more in demand right now than others. However, the historical trend towards mass global prosperity is likely to exert pressure on the demand side for some time to come, barring a calamity.

Within each commodity, there is something called the "roll" return. This comes from the fact that, in most cases, the future price of a commodity is higher than the price today (the price today is called the "spot" price). This is because of storage costs, insurance costs, and interest rate costs. Why should someone go to the trouble of storing frozen orange juice when he could more easily put his money in the bank and get interest on it? The buyers need to be compensated for their service. For example, frozen orange juice concentrate will be cheapest the day of delivery (when it is most plentiful) and then rise in price over time as these other costs are added, right up until the next delivery date when the cycle starts all over again.

Of course, other factors like good or bad weather will also affect the price along the way. The strategy of rolling our commodities positions over, buying when they are cheap and selling as they rise in value closer to expiration, has usually added to returns, although this strategy can also turn against us if prices fall.

Finally, if we own a bunch of different commodity futures contracts in equal amounts, there can be (and in fact has been) an added return from the discipline of selling high and buying low as we rebalance our portfolio over time. Individual commodity prices are volatile and have low correlations to each other, leaving plenty of room to generate a portfolio diversification premium by periodically selling the ones that have gone up and using the proceeds to shore up positions in the others that are lagging.

Do Commodities Add Value to a Portfolio?

If we believe that commodities have almost any real positive expected return, they are going to have a place in our portfolio. Why?

― ∽ ―

If you believe that commodities have almost any real positive expected return, they are going to have a place in your portfolio.

- Commodities *generally* have low to negative correlations with both stocks and bonds.
- Commodities are *generally* a hedge against inflation, including inflation shocks.
- Commodities' negative correlation to the stock market can appear precisely when we need it most: during recessions and crashes. But not always.

Commodities did brilliantly during the stagflation of the 1970s, when they beat inflation by about 10 percentage points a year. They have tended to shine when stocks were having bad years.

However, what is foremost on investors' minds these days is the liquidity panic of 2008, when commodities let us down. Investors who expected a big diversification benefit from commodities found the earth crumbling beneath their feet during the massive global deleveraging. The recency of this lesson and the magnitude of its pain should not blind us to the potential long-term benefits of using commodities in a portfolio. The next crisis is unlikely to be just like the last one.

According to one published paper on the subject, from 1970 to 2004, during which time the prices of individual commodities were more or less flat, a composite commodity index would have returned about 4 to 6 percentage points above the return on T-bills. This kind of return is enough to justify a meaningful allocation to most portfolios.

While the exact composition of commodity returns remains a puzzle, a 2006 Ibbotson Associates (a division of Morningstar) article on commodity returns concludes, "We believe most of these return drivers are likely to persist in the future and contribute to an inherent return for commodities." At the same time, we have to acknowledge that it is difficult to get a fix on their long-term expected risks, returns, or correlations to everything else.

How Do We Invest in It?

You may have a can of coffee in the kitchen, some gas in your car, and a nickel in your pocket—these are specific products made from commodities. But even if you have a garage mahal, it is not going to be practical for you to store bales of cotton and bushels of corn. You might be able to store gold bars, but that is not without danger, either.

Some people think the best way to own commodities is by buying commodity producers: mining companies, oil companies, agricultural companies, and so on. This is wrong. Commodity producers are a hybrid between a commodity and a stock, with much higher correlations to the stock market than to the underlying commodities. You already own stocks. Buying commodity producers surrenders much of the diversifying power that was the reason for owning commodities in the first place. It's better to cut out the middleman.

Another bad idea is to open an account with a commodity trading advisor. You object: Hillary Clinton did and turned $1,000 into a tidy $99,540 in 10 months with no experience whatsoever. Well, we suppose you can, too—if your spouse is governor and no one is watching. Otherwise, stay away from these shark-infested waters. You will be playing on margin in a casino where the fees and commissions are steep. We will have more to say about futures accounts later, but for now there is a better way.

Fortunately, commodities have been neatly packaged into ordinary mutual funds and exchange-traded funds. These funds are passive vehicles that track the performance of some commodity benchmark index. They are "fully collateralized," which means our exposure to the underlying commodities is not leveraged.

There are several good funds to consider:

- The *PowerShares DB Commodity Index Tracking Fund* (ticker: DBC, 0.85 percent expense ratio): This fund tracks the Deutsche Bank Commodity Index, which passively follows a rules-based allocation to 14 important commodities. The fund provides collateral for its position using 3-month T-bills. A word of caution: This index significantly overweights the energy segment at 55 percent, which means its performance relies heavily on the price of oil. When oil goes up, this fund outperforms the others, but when oil goes down it will underperform. That also makes it more volatile than other commodity index funds.

One important issue is that it hands you a K-1 for tax reporting purposes. Most owners will simplify their tax lives by housing DBC inside an IRA or tax-qualified account. Even then, the K-1 income can be taxed if it generates more than $1,000 of "unrelated business taxable income," which the fund will assiduously try to avoid.

- The *iPath Dow Jones-AIG Commodity Index Total Return ETN* (ticker: DJP, 0.75 percent expense ratio): The iPath note paces the Dow Jones-UBS Commodity Index, which tracks 19 different commodities and caps the weighting to each sector, so it is more diversified. However, the fund itself is not a claim on a bunch of commodities but rather a bank note from Barclays Bank PLC. It generates 1099 income rather than K-1 income, making it better suited for a taxable account than the Deutsche Bank Commodity Index Tracking Fund.

The trade-off is that it introduces counterparty risk: The fund is backed by Barclays Bank.

- The *Elements Rogers International Commodity ETN* (ticker: RJI, 0.75 percent expense ratio): This fund is also an exchange-traded note, this time from the Swedish Export Credit Corporation. This structure avoids the K-1 partnership form that can complicate your taxes. It also offers the broadest and most diversified exposure of any of the commodity funds, with allocations to 35 different commodities ranked annually by Rogers according to their importance in international commerce.

- The *DFA Commodity Strategy Portfolio* (ticker: DCMSX): Investors who use Dimensional Funds-affiliated advisors will want to consider DFA's new Commodity Strategy Portfolio. It does not track any particular index (but has similar sector weights to the Dow Jones-UBS Commodity Index) and follows DFA's characteristic low-temperature trading strategy. The commodities futures contracts and swap agreements are collateralized by investments in DFA's short-term investment-grade bond fund. This is the cheapest commodity exposure you can get, with a management fee of 0.30 percent and an overall expense ratio capped at 0.55 percent, although your advisor's fees will be on top of this.

There are many other commodity funds out there. *The PIMCO Commodity Real Return Strategy* (ticker: PCRAX, among several share classes) is also supposed to track the Dow Jones-UBS Commodity Index, and puts the collateral into a PIMCO actively managed bond portfolio. If you like the PIMCO approach and you don't have an advisor, you can get it for less by buying the *Harbor Commodity Real Return Fund* (ticker: HACMX), which has the same manager. By now there are many commodity sub-index funds that track the performance of individual commodities, but we don't recommend these unless you are some kind of expert, which, frankly, we doubt.

Later on we talk about how much to buy in the way of a commodity index fund. In the next chapter we want to turn you on to the next "real" asset class, real estate.

The Alternative Reality

While not everyone agrees, we think a small allocation to commodities is a good idea that should improve the risk/return profile of your portfolio. The presence of several good commodity index funds makes this asset class easy to access for all investors.

Conventional
Alternatives II:
Real Estate

~

In Real Estate We Trust

WEALTH USED TO BE SYNONYMOUS WITH REAL ESTATE ("real" means royal in Spanish). Whether you were King, Queen or just the Duke, Duke, Duke of Earl, your wealth consisted principally of land. *The Little Book of Royal Investing*, had it existed back in those days, would have advised you to get land and more land, since land was synonymous with wealth. Those without land—nearly everyone else alive at the time—led a hand-to-mouth existence.

The industrial revolution changed all that, catapulting us into a modern world where we have reached a point at which people need to be reminded that yes, real estate is an important asset class to include in their portfolios. Agricultural assets have given way to industrial assets and the financial assets that are predicated upon them, such as stocks and bonds.

There are two types of real estate: *residential* and *commercial*. By residential, we mean your house. Your house may well be your biggest asset. If you haven't done so already, please buy a house. Houses are great—just ask Ben, who owns a surprising number of them. The U.S. government makes owning real estate too good a deal to pass up, especially if you can afford it. However, do not overbuy. As Adam Smith pointed out in *The Wealth of Nations* (1776), a personal residence is essentially an item of consumption, not an investment, alternative or otherwise. If you keep your home for a long time, it will turn into a significant asset, although beyond the free rent (a considerable advantage) it only becomes useful to you as money when you cash it in. Unless you sell it, downsize, and spend the difference, your paid-off house primarily benefits your heirs.

For more of our deep thoughts on this topic, check out our previous *Little Book of Bulletproof Investing,* which contains a chapter on residential real estate. Perhaps you are considering buying a vacation home in Aspen and renting it out so that you will end up with a free house, paid for by renters, while you are able to take free ski vacations for the next 30 years. Read our other *Little Book* first. (When Ben tells audiences the story of his home renovation-at-a-distance in Aspen, it moves them to tears. At least, it moves Ben to tears.)

The point is, even though you own your house, it is not really an investment in the same way your stocks and bonds are. You still can benefit from additional exposure to real estate in your portfolio.

Which brings us to property type number two: commercial real estate. This is everything that is not a house. Say you're walking down the street and see a skyscraper. This would be an example of commercial real estate. You might want to buy it. Immediately, though, there's a problem. It's expensive.

Only rich people—or institutional investors—buy commercial real estate directly. For them, it's not a hobby. They have to perform due diligence on the buildings they are buying. It's not smart to buy just one—they need a whole portfolio of properties diversified by type and geography. They have to oversee their entire real estate portfolio, buying and selling properties as it strikes their fancy. Then they need to manage the properties: Collect the rent, fix the radiator, patch the paint, lay the carpet, call the plumber. For a long time, only very large investors dabbled in this market.

This changed on September 14, 1960, when President Eisenhower signed the Cigar Excise Tax Extension. Under the wrapper, this bill contained the Real Estate Investment Trust Act—giving birth to REITs, as they are known. This act was usefully modified by the Tax Reform Act of 1986, which allowed these trusts to both own and manage real estate in one vertically-integrated company. With the stroke of a pen, commercial real estate became available to everyone as an alternative investing option.

How Do Investors Use REITs?

Real Estate Investment Trusts are publicly traded companies that own and operate office buildings, apartment complexes, and the like. To qualify as a REIT under the Internal Revenue Code, the company must invest at least 75 percent of its total assets in qualifying real estate assets and derive at least 75 percent of its gross income either from rents or interest on mortgages. In addition, a REIT must distribute at least 90 percent of its taxable income annually to its shareholders as dividends. As a result, most

REITs pay no corporate tax, as the taxes are effectively passed along to shareholders.

The REIT structure solves the problems that kept ordinary retail investors at bay. REITs are liquid, diversified, and professionally managed. This is a big deal. Try selling an industrial park and it may take you a while, but you can sell a REIT that specializes in industrial properties with a click of a mouse.

REITs are run with oversight from a board of directors, and are subject to market discipline as they trade on the major stock exchanges throughout the world. They can be acquired for a few dollars in commissions instead of by hiring a Realtor. Little wonder REITs have mushroomed.

In the United States, there are two types of REITs:

1. Equity REITs, which own income-producing properties.
2. Mortgage REITs, which invest in loans secured by either residential or commercial real estate.

In this chapter, we talk about equity REITs, since mortgage REITs are better thought of as credit (that is, bond-like) instruments. Mortgage REITs have their own unique characteristics. They are generally long-term loans that pay an above-average coupon to compensate for the fact that they will be repaid at exactly the wrong time, when interest rates are falling. We leave it to others to analyze them.

How Do REITs Work?

Here is the secret to how equity REITs work: Landlords collect rents from tenants and distribute them to shareholders. The sustainability of this business model is what makes being a landlord the second oldest profession.

Someday, a worldwide Communist revolution may abolish private property and usher in a worker's paradise. Until then, the idea of landlords collecting rent is about as durable a business proposition as can be imagined. If you don't believe us, try not paying your rent next month and watch what happens.

The premise of landlords collecting rent is about as durable a business proposition as can be imagined.

Do REITs Add Value to a Portfolio?

Owning REITs no longer makes you cool all by itself. REITs are such a common alternative investment that—as with commodities—they are not really alternative anymore.

As investments, REITs have several beguiling features:

- An equity structure
- Assets that are real, that is, should keep up with inflation
- Cash flows like a long-term bond
- Returns that are leveraged

The fact that the real estate is set inside an equity wrapper and traded alongside other stocks on the stock exchange means that it is going to behave something like a stock. The fact that REITs represent pass-through vehicles for the rents they collect makes them something like a bond , or a curious cocktail of stock plus bond plus real estate. REITs will behave like stocks and bonds, losing value when interest rates rise and gaining value when they fall, other things being equal.

Did we mention that REITs are leveraged? These managers aren't dumb; they don't usually pay all cash for their properties. They borrow money to finance them, typically to the tune of about 40 to 50 percent. This is less leverage than is used on most commercial real estate, and less than most people use when buying their houses.

In practice, REITs have produced high returns with high volatility. From 1990 to 2005, they had a mean return of 11.4 percent per year and an annual standard deviation of nearly 25 percent. The first decade of the 21st century was called a "lost decade" for equities, but the Vanguard Real Estate Index fund (ticker: VGSIX) was up 10.3 percent over that 10-year stretch, which is not great but is still 11.4 percent better than stocks. Before you back up the truck, remember that REITs were down 38 percent when Krypton exploded in 2008— even more than the stock market. They diversified you down, exactly when you needed them to pull you up.

Just because an investment doesn't perform perfectly doesn't mean we should avoid it. Berkshire Hathaway stock—one of the greatest investments of all time—has, on three occasions, lost half of its value. There were other bad times for stocks when REITs were in there pitching. During the inflation of the 1970s, REITs were the single best performing asset class. REITs generally have a low to moderate correlation to the rest of the stock market (in the 0.40 to 0.70 range, although the correlation rose to 0.79 in 2008).

Notably, REITs contain two hedges against inflation: rents and property. Many leases contain clauses allowing for periodic inflation adjustments. During inflation, investors tend to shift from paper assets to real assets, driving up property values. REITs add tremendously to a portfolio's inflation-fighting ability. Consider that the baby boom generation is now on the cusp of retirement, desperately in need of a rich income stream, and that inflation is a retiree's worst enemy, and you will understand how an allocation to REITs is justifiable even if their performance in the future turns out to be less exceptional than it has been in the past.

How Do We Invest in It?

One way to invest in commercial real estate is to buy a small apartment building in your hometown. This hobby is not going to be as much fun as it sounds. Your authors have already confessed to incidents from their own younger days as tenants when they were guilty of incurring a landlord's displeasure, including the notorious affair of the second-story waterbed where the unattended hose that was filling the mattress slipped out, filling the apartment building with water instead.

If you, landlord, are up to these challenges, God bless you. You are banking on your sweat equity and local knowledge of real estate conditions to come out ahead. Against this, though, you are concentrating your real estate eggs in your hometown basket, which may or may not turn out to be a great idea. It is an added risk for which you are not being compensated.

There is an easier way, and that way is to buy REITs. You can always try to pick individual REITs if that is your passion, but your life will be simplified by picking a mutual fund that samples the entire REIT universe. All the arguments against individual stock picking apply to REITs as well, and the REIT index funds outperform the actively managed funds by similar margins. Buying a REIT index fund can offer us a small piece of virtually every publicly traded property on the planet. This diversifies away all the idiosyncratic risk, and does it for peanuts.

There are lots of excellent REIT mutual funds that charge low expenses and give investors access to the entire REIT asset class. Which ones to choose? Once again, the world bifurcates into investors who use investment advisors and those who do it themselves. Those with advisors will gravitate toward the passive offerings from Dimensional Funds, domestic (ticker: DFREX), international (ticker: DFITX), or both in one global fund (ticker: DFGEX).

For those going it alone, the many retail REIT index funds have subtle differences but their similarities are even greater, so you should shop by price. You can't beat Vanguard's MSCI REIT index exchange-traded fund (ticker: VNQ), which charges an astonishingly low 0.13 percent a year, along with its international REIT cousin (ticker: VNQI), which charges 0.35 percent.

Since REITs are pass-through structures, they leave the taxes to be paid directly by the shareholders. Only about 40 percent of the dividends are taxed at the lower dividend tax rate; the rest are taxed as ordinary income. This makes REITs an ideal candidate for your IRA, annuity, 401(k), or other tax-deferred account (although future changes to the tax law may alter this opinion). Because REITs also hold out the prospect of significant capital appreciation, they should be some of the first things you load into your Roth IRA.

The Alternative Reality

No controversy here: There is widespread agreement that portfolios benefit from a separate allocation to REITs, in spite of the fact that REITs are already present in equity market index funds.

Why? Some say it's because the total stock market weightings do not take into account the vast real estate holdings in private hands, so that a special allocation is required to more accurately mirror the market-wide holdings of all participants. Who knows? The availability of many excellent REIT index funds makes this now-conventional alternative easy to include in your portfolio.

Chapter Seven

The Ultimate Alternative Investments

Hedge Fundamentals

HAVING COVERED CONVENTIONAL INVESTMENTS, plus some alternative investments we don't love as well as some that we do, we now turn to the alternative alternatives that will be our main focus from here on: hedge funds.

Say Whaa...?

What is a hedge fund? AQR Capital's Cliff Asness wrote the definition that no one has topped: "Hedge funds are investment pools that are relatively unconstrained in what they do. They are relatively unregulated (for now), charge very high fees, will not necessarily give you your money back when you want it, and will generally not tell you what they do. They are supposed to make money all the time, and when they fail at this, their investors redeem and go to someone else who has recently been making money. Every three or four years they deliver a one-in-a-hundred year flood. They are generally run for rich people in Geneva, Switzerland, by rich people in Greenwich, Connecticut."

A hedge fund is an alternative investment vehicle available only to wealthy investors, such as institutions and accredited investors presumed to be financially numerate because they possess significant assets (currently defined as those with over $1 million in financial assets or who make more than $250,000 a year). They are not currently regulated by the U.S. Securities and Exchange Commission (SEC), a financial industry oversight entity, as mutual funds are. However, more regulation for hedge funds may be coming.

The popularity of these alternative investment vehicles—first created in 1949—has waxed and waned over the years. Hedge funds proliferated during the 1960s and again during the market boom in the 2000s, but many closed in the wake of the 2007 and 2008 credit crisis. With the decline of private clubs, hedge funds have become the new country clubs.

How do hedge funds try to produce "absolute returns" (a marketing slogan rather than a description of any investment reality) that are disconnected from those in the stock and bond markets? Partly it is because they invest in alternative assets and partly it is because they follow alternative investment strategies. Most stock investors buy shares of companies hoping that the stream of earnings will rise and support a higher price when they sell the stock. Most bond investors are looking for a steady payout over time and a return of principal when the bond matures. If the bond increases in value along the way, so much the better. As discussed earlier, those are the basic ideas behind stock and bond investing.

Hedge funds are more complicated. If they were simple, everybody would be running one—although sometimes it seems like everybody *is* running one. The idea is not for you to become a hedge fund manager yourself, but to learn how you can use the same alternative strategies that hedge funds use, even if you are not an accredited investor (yet). The downside is that we can't just tell a few jokes and breeze through this part. If you're not already familiar with how hedge funds work, you are going to have to put on your thinking cap and follow along. Hedge funds are more complicated than a game of Tic-Tac-Toe, but fortunately they are not string theory, either.

Exploiting Market Anomalies

Today's hedge funds have been made possible by several developments.

1. The ability to go *short*—bet that a stock price will go down—expanded the fund manager's domain of operations beyond that of the traditional long-only investor.

2. By being allowed to go long and/or short on similar assets, hedge funds were able to neutralize the overall market risk. Taking the rest of the stock market out of the picture (having a correlation to the stock market of close to zero) put the managers' own virtuosic skill on display, unlinked to the usual tie-in with the stock market.

3. With the market risk canceled out, managers could more safely *leverage* their trades. They could borrow money to make more money on each transaction (but, if they were wrong, lose more, too).

4. Computers and stock market databases suddenly made it possible to analyze massive amounts of data in real time.

5. New markets in futures and derivatives made it possible to target precise elements of risk and reward that these models sought to exploit.

6. Computers made it possible to trade super efficiently, executing large trades with lightning rapidity by using direct market access instead of via the usual gang of brokers.

7. Trading commissions were driven down to a vanishing point, which made it possible to execute strategies of borderline profitability, promoting them to acceptable profitability once leverage was applied.

8. As the rewards from investment management went through the roof, the brightest (if not always the best) were drawn into high-paying careers in finance. People who otherwise would have become doctors or engineers started running hedge funds instead.

Essentially, hedge funds exploit small market anomalies, the sea shells left on the beach by the ocean of efficient markets. They find trades where the upside potential appears greater than the downside risk. They buy large blocks of stocks at a discount by coming up with cash (supplying *liquidity*) when a big sale would otherwise hammer down the price. They take on certain arcane risks that others do not want or cannot take. They trade against institutions such as central banks and others who sometimes act solely for policy or political reasons. (More on this in due course.)

~

Hedge funds exploit small market anomalies, the sea shells left on the beach by the ocean of efficient markets.

Another feature that cuts across many hedge funds might be called serious research. As we mentioned, these funds are often run by super bright people who put in long hours making pinpointed studies and doing very careful analysis. This gives them an edge. You might watch a DVD and think about buying Netflix. These people have already done the equivalent of a Ph.D. dissertation on Netflix, and they are the ones you are trading against. In fact, they want you to play. Sit down, we'll deal you in—can we get you a drink?

Ben once met a man who had had the terrible misfortune to be imprisoned and tortured in an Eastern European Communist country. When Ben sympathized, the man brushed it off. "Actually, it wasn't so bad. The torturer was a civil servant. To him it was just a job. He had a lot of people to torture and not enough time to torture them. My appointment was late Friday afternoon, when he was more interested in getting home to his wife and kids."

Professional money managers are a lot like that Communist civil servant. They are doing a job, but not really trading as if their lives depended on it as hedge fund managers do.

However, the purpose of hedge funds is not to do God's work. It is not to allocate risk. It is not to aid in price discovery or to supply liquidity. It is not to narrow price spreads or smooth discontinuities or reduce market inefficiencies. The purpose of hedge funds is to make money.

The Secret Sauce

Most sensible investment writing necessarily focuses on what *not* to do. The big casino of Wall Street wants to lure you in, divert and amuse you with invest-o-tainment, keep you stupid, and get you playing. In this environment, all the good advice is defensive. Don't play. Don't drink. Don't pay attention to them. Buy an index fund and get out of Vegas.

Phil's nephew Chris DeMuth, Jr.—manager of Rangeley Capital (the only hedge fund both your authors own)—points out that using hedge funds takes us from a passive ducking-for-cover to an active stance. Instead of just keeping our heads down while other investors get picked off, we look for opportunities to exploit and fire back.

Where do these opportunities arise? From various obscure corners and back alleys of the market. One common source is the "agency" problem: the fact that agencies acting on behalf of others tend to put their own interests first. Consider the initial public offering (IPO) of a new closed-end fund.

Closed-end funds are simple baskets of stocks or bonds. They exist primarily because they provide a one-time money-making opportunity for those selling them. The brokers get paid an 8 percent commission. Their clients are patsies who end up paying $25 for exactly $23 worth of securities. Because no one has any interest in touting these products after the IPO has passed, they usually drift even lower in price, to discounts of 20 percent or more to the net asset value of the underlying securities. This is when hedge funds buy them from the now disgusted buyers, who simply want the pain off their statements. Where agency problems abound, hedge funds are there to capitalize on them. (Don't try this at home. It only works if someone has enough money to compel a liquidation.)

Another source of opportunity is the "narrow mandate" problem. For example, there is not much mystery about which stocks are going to be added to the Russell 2000 index of small U.S. companies each June. Being added to the index means the stock will get a pop, since all the funds licensing the index are forced to add it to their portfolios. Since everyone is clamoring to buy a thinly traded stock at the same time, the price is artificially bid up. The index investors overpay, foolishly handing money to the hedge funds who bought these stocks on the cheap before the announcement. The world has institutions who sometimes must act for policy reasons rather than for economic advantage, and hedge funds lie in wait to take the other side of these trades.

A third source of opportunity is simply when people need cash. If you need cash today, you will sell at a discount to get it. When people need to unload blocks of securities for any reason, hedge funds are there with deep pockets to help them out—at a price. (We're going to talk more about this later, but there are merger and acquisition funds and these often can be gold mines.)

These are the kinds of actions hedge fund managers can take that you probably can't, unless you are a hedge fund manager yourself and this is your specialty.

Illusion versus Reality

Since we'll be talking a lot about these alternative strategies in the chapters ahead, we need to start by clearing the air. A lot of ridiculous myths have grown up around hedge funds. Believe it or not, many otherwise intelligent people still believe these abominable lies.

Myth: Hedge Funds Charge High Fees

Good grief, man, do you know what a 500-foot yacht costs these days? What about important paintings by

Van Gogh and Pollock? How about renting Versailles, as hedge fund manager Ken Griffin did for his wedding?

Then there's the high cost of entertaining. Hedge fund manager Stephen Partridge-Hicks chartered a jet to fly 150 of his closest friends to Morocco for a James Bond-themed party. A particular highlight was staging a movie scene featuring himself (who else?) as 007—complete with fire eaters, dancing monkeys, a submarine, and a fly-by from Russian MiGs. This kind of tailgate party doesn't come cheap.

You can't expect a fund manager to swim in these waters if he gives away his services for free. Throw in a private jet, mansions in Greenwich designed by world-renowned architects, sports cars, polo ponies, trophy wives, dogs, and supermodel girlfriends, and it adds up. When J.P. Morgan died in 1913 and left an estate worth $80 million, John D. Rockefeller observed, "And to think we thought him a wealthy man." Remember that what seems expensive to you, dear reader, may only be pocket change to a fund manager, who, at the absolute top of the pile, can make $5 billion in a single year—a multiple of J.P. Morgan's entire estate in constant dollars.

It's easy to forget that, despite all the money sloshing around their bank accounts, these hedge fund managers are plain folks like you and me. According to one newspaper story about the housing market in the Hamptons, due to the recent widespread hardship, "There is tremendous pressure on the part of those people who could write a check and buy a [weekend] house for $15 million to $20 million not to do it at this point in time." Another article on vacation travel emphasizes that when hedge fund managers take time off (perhaps on the featured $300,000 one-week trip to Paris), "They want to get back to basics."

Where does all the money come from to pay for these luxuries/necessities? Why, from the high fees they charge, of course. While an S&P 500 index fund might charge 6/100ths of a percent in management fees, hedge funds famously charge "2 & 20." That is, they rake off 2 percent of your money every year for expenses (coffee, pens, printer cartridges, etc.—in some cases, research), and they also take a mere 20 percent of all profits above some hurdle rate as a performance fee, like the "Royal Fifth" of all the gold the Conquistadors took from the Indians and paid as tribute to the King of Spain.

Then, in addition to charging generous fees, hedge fund managers get to keep more of what they rake in. Do you perhaps pay federal income taxes at high marginal rates? You fool! They don't. Since their performance fees are structured as a percentage of the fund's profits, much of their income is taxed as long-term capital gains. Not only do they earn more than we do up front, most of their income is sheltered from marginal IRS tax rates.

Yes, it's pretty cool to be them.

Myth: Performance Fees Pit the Interests of Hedge Fund Managers against Those of Their Own Customers

Critics claim that the asymmetrical nature of the performance fee distorts the incentives of hedge fund managers. Managers share in the profits—but not in the pain—of their customers. They take 20 percent off the top, but, strange to say, are not volunteering to give 20 percent back in a down year.

Say you are a fund manager and it's December 15th. Your fund is below its hurdle rate for the year (the amount below which no performance fee is granted). This means Santa Claus isn't going to be depositing a fat bonus check in your stocking. And all your wife can talk about is how well her friend's husbands (all hedge fund managers) are doing. Have you lost your mojo, she wonders. That tenderness like before in her fingertips? It's gone, gone, gone.

Then, a hugely risky deal crosses your desk. If it pays off, it could redeem your whole year, especially with enough leverage. The bonus check will come in after all. You'll be able to hold your head high at the New Year's party, while your wife shows off her new diamond and emerald drop earrings. You've brought back that lovin' feeling.

Of course, there's an even bigger chance the whole deal will blow up in your face. Time for a Hail Mary. If you lose, it's not exactly your problem, now, is it? Sure, your investors will be mad, but even if they want out, their money is locked up, and by the time they can get it back you will probably have turned things around so they won't leave after all.

You sit at your desk, weighing the choice: a possible big bonus, or the certainty of no bonus. Are you a player, or just . . . a loser?

Believe it or not, critics have been insulting enough to suggest that a hedge fund manager, confronted with these circumstances, might roll the dice on a risky deal just to get his bonus—mere money. This completely overlooks the selfless, altruistic side of human nature. Look at Gandhi. Look at St. Francis. Who's to say that, behind the security gates at his Greenwich compound, your hedge fund manager isn't wandering naked through the garden preaching peace and love to the birds and squirrels?

Myth: Hedge Fund Operators Abuse "High-Water" Marks

Some hedge funds have a "high-water" mark, which means that managers don't collect a penny of their performance fees unless the fund is over its previous high level. This seems like a fair shake for investors.

Yet, some peevish faultfinders suggest that this sets up the same perverse inventive that we saw above: It just shifts the goal line from the hurdle rate to the high-water mark. It rewards reckless behavior rather than prudence.

These critics are wrong. There is no need whatsoever for a hedge fund manager to swing for the fences when he is below his high-water mark. Why should he, when it is far easier to just close the fund and open a new one? Presto—the high-water mark disappears.

For example, when John Meriwether's hedge fund Long Term Capital Management exploded, he opened JWM Partners. This fund closed when it was down 44 percent. His solution? Start a new fund, JM Partners. The high-water marks present no obstacle to success for the audacious hedge fund manager who is willing to try, try, try again.

Myth: Hedge Fund Performance Isn't What It's Cracked Up to Be

As we mentioned, hedge funds are structured as limited partnerships or offshore corporations so there is presently no reporting requirement. Databases exist, but since reporting is voluntary, critics argue that there may be a slight tendency to overreport the good news and bury the bad.

How might this exaggeration creep into the performance numbers? Let's say you start five hedge funds.

After a year, four of them have lost money, but the fifth has done well. Which one are you going to talk about when they call to ask you about your returns? Now you have one fund tracked by the hedge fund databases. The following year it does terribly and all your investors leave. What happens next? The fund can be deleted from the database, as if it never existed.

These issues—known as survivorship and backfill bias—are difficult to eliminate. As a result, hedge fund returns are overstated.

To get a better handle on what the actual returns have been, researchers from Ibbotson Associates put the data through a wringer and subtracted the fees from the equation. Their conclusion: From 1995 through 2009, hedge funds had a compound return of about 7.6 percent annually over this period. This compares to an annualized return of 8 percent from the S&P 500 Index.

But why focus on the negative? If you don't correct for these biases, and you don't subtract the fees, the returns shoot up to a whopping 15 percent—a much prettier number.

Myth: Hedge Funds Don't Hedge

Hedge funds first became popular because of their dazzling performances. People invested with them because they wanted to get rich.

Over time, however, it became apparent that not all children in Lake Wobegon were above average. While a few funds grabbed the headlines, most did not. It began to be doubted whether hedge funds in aggregate outperformed even the conventional stock benchmarks, as the Ibbotson study showed. Fortunately, hedge fund managers had a fallback position. Okay, maybe they didn't outperform, but at least they hedged. In other words, they delivered returns that were meaningfully uncorrelated to those from the stock market. As a friend remarked when he showed us his quarterly letter from his manager, "This is a true hedge fund. It manages to lose money in both good markets and bad."

Now, critics have begun to dispute even the hedge part. Will they stop at nothing?

Hedge funds returns, they suggest, are positively correlated to the general level of economic activity in society. For example, when stocks are up, that is also when there are a lot of mergers and acquisition going on, which makes a fertile arena for some hedge funds. Then, as volatility falls during a bull market, hedge funds get sidelined from their bets, and are forced into strategies that are more highly correlated with the equity markets. The strategies become crowded, diluted, and less hedgy. As more money flows in and gets compounded by leverage, this completes a positive feedback loop forcing stocks up by the sheer pressure of hedge fund buying at the margins.

Of course, once this luau ends, all these factors get thrown into reverse. The result is remarkably equity-like performance from expensive hedge fund investing.

But, wait! Critics suggest that there may even be something more sinister going on. If you wonder about the price of Microsoft, you can find out to the penny 24 hours a day. Hedge funds, however, take positions in a lot of securities that are priced infrequently. When the end of the month comes and they have to report prices for the portfolio, there may be no recent trades to examine. This is when the professional manager is called upon to exercise his seasoned judgment in determining the prices, and therefore the returns, of his fund. Researchers looking at the Dow Jones Credit Suisse Hedge Fund index from 1994 to 2000 found a correlation to the S&P 500 stock index of 0.52 using the prices that managers reported, but 0.63 using the actual prices as determined later. It is possible that the manager may be subliminally aware that all his investors are counting on him for good results that are uncorrelated to the stock market. Under these circumstances, there may be some slight unconscious tendency toward telling people the prices they want to hear, just to smooth the ride a bit. After all, what's the harm in using stale or stage-managed prices as long as everyone is having fun?

Ibbotson Associates have calculated that the correlation between the Hedge Fund Research Institute (HFRI) composite index and the S&P 500 index from 1990 to 2007 was 0.70. Looking at the correlations between hedge fund indexes and the MSCI All-World index of global stocks from 1994 to 2009, we again see correlations in the 0.65 to 0.76 range. There is also the looming prospect that hedge fund correlations to the stock market are increasing over time. Hedge fund investors pay a lot for a product that looks like it has derived half its performance from the stock market. Meanwhile, over this same period, Real Estate Investment Trusts (REITs) had a correlation of 0.51 and commodities actually had a negative correlation. Investors could have found lower correlations and better hedges far more cheaply in their own backyards.

Myth: Hedge Funds Are Too Expensive to Offer Diversification

It has been suggested that only rich people can afford the diversification benefits of hedge funds. Poppycock. Since there are basically 10 hedge fund strategies, and most hedge funds will let you in the door with $1,000,000, all you need is $10,000,000 to diversify into each one—assuming that you are comfortable using only one manager per strategy. Probably, three managers per strategy would be better. If you have $30,000,000 to spend on hedge funds, and you further assume that hedge funds comprise 20 percent of your investment budget, you can have a well diversified portfolio with a liquid net worth of only $150,000,000. What's the problem?

However, we don't want to forget about the "little people." Here's a tip that will get you a diversified portfolio of hedge funds for as little as $250,000 or $500,000. Buy a hedge fund "fund-of-funds." True, you'll have to pay another layer of fees on top of the hedge funds fees already in the fund. You'll also have to do your own due diligence on the fund-of-hedge-fund managers, which is not as easy as it sounds. Funds-of-funds got quite a black eye in 2008 when it became apparent that a number of them were feeders to Bernie Madoff. Until recently, the fund-of-funds approach is the only way ordinary high-net-worth investors could get exposure to a diversified set of hedge fund strategies, and it still may be the only path to hedge fund alpha for most—if you can find a good one. Just make sure your advisor is not investing in the *next* Bernie Madoff.

Myth: Hedge Funds Are Illiquid

People say that hedge funds are illiquid—that you can't get your money out when you want it—but that is another falsehood. As a client, all you have to do to get your money back is write a letter to the fund manager three months in advance and you'll get a check at the end of the quarter. For example, if you want your money out at the end of the year, write your manager by the end of September. Wait until October 1 and you won't get your money until the end of March. Some funds have variations on this policy. For example, some will only let you take your money out once a year.

Did we say get a check? That's not quite true. If you are redeeming your entire position, you might only get 90 percent back. They have to hold back 10 percent until the year-end accounting is finished, in April of the following year—even if you redeemed at the end of March this year.

Get cash? Well, that depends. If the fund is liquidating, you may be paid in kind instead—for example, in illiquid securities from bankrupt companies. Who knows? These could turn out to be quite valuable under the right circumstances. Normally, though, you get cash.

If the fund is doing well you should have no trouble getting your money out. However, if your manager is in the middle of some monster transaction and feels it would make the other fund shareholders dyspeptic to liquidate your stakes, he can "gate" your money and lock it up until a more convenient time. This usually only happens during bad times, but you probably didn't really need it right away. If this happens, you will usually get your money back within one to three years.

People who complain about hedge funds locking up their money fail to consider the opposite case. Far from being illiquid, there are successful funds that have returned money to investors once the manager has struck it rich and no longer wants to carry the other investors on his back. If the fund manager feels that he is making less money because everyone else's money is weighing down his performance, he won't hesitate to return your money to you precisely when you don't want it. Then you can watch from the sidelines as the fund you helped put on its feet takes off without you.

Myth: Hedge Funds Are Risky

What—hedge fund risky? That is like saying nuclear energy is risky just because a few atom bombs have gone off here and there. Hedge funds are lightly regulated the same way that *Playboy* centerfolds are lightly dressed. Sure, they use strategies that are so arcane only a computer can comprehend them. Sure, they can lever up these strategies 25-to-1. Isn't it the business of life to be dangerous?

~

Hedge funds are lightly regulated the same way that *Playboy* centerfolds are lightly dressed.

These naysayers are probably thinking about Long Term Capital Management. Or Amaranth. Or Peloton

Partners. Or Carlyle Capital. Or Bayou Management. Or Marin Capital. Or Bernie Madoff. Notice how they never talk about all the funds that don't blow up. The ones who don't trade on criminally obtained information. The ones where the FBI doesn't knock on their doors. And anyway, Madoff wasn't running a hedge fund, he was running a Ponzi scheme.

All you need to do is some simple due diligence. A 20-page checklist of questions will get the discussion rolling. You could hire someone else to do it for you, but this begs the question: How do you do the due diligence on them?

It Gets Worse

As if all this weren't bad enough, the funds we want won't even let us in. The famous hedge funds we read about are all closed to new investors. This leaves us like street urchins with our noses pressed against the frosted windowpane, watching the Norman Rockwellesque Thanksgiving banquet going on inside the club.

Talk about bad luck—here we are, wanting to sex up our portfolios, willing to forgive these managers for their sins, and now they refuse to take our money.

Admittedly, it looks discouraging. Is there any hope?

No, there is none at all.

Wait a minute—of course there is.

The Alternative Reality

We might as well concede up front that there are numerous reasons to treat hedge fund investing with a healthy amount of skepticism.

We concede it.

On the other hand, if you are a very high net worth investor with an inside track on a good fund, and you have done your 75 to 100 hours of due diligence, and are willing to take the risks along with the rewards, that fund might be just the thing for you.

If you are not a very high net worth investor, though, there is still a way for you to get some of the same benefits.

Chapter Eight

So Why Invest in Hedge Funds?

~

Okay, We Lied

IF ALL OF THE PREVIOUS SO-CALLED MYTHS ARE VALID reasons to be wary of investing in hedge funds, there must be some pretty good arguments on the other side to explain why professional investors stand by them. Pensions, institutions, endowments, and tax-exempt organizations use hedge funds for anywhere from 10 to 25 percent (depending on which study you read) of their investment allocation, while retail investors like us—who also would like to make a dollar if we could—have close to zero percent in the game. What's an investor to do?

Final Answer

Okay, we're going to tell you.

But before we do, we have to come clean. First, we admit that hedge funds in aggregate are probably not going to "beat the market." Any given year, some funds will beat the stock market by a spectacular amount. Over time, however, many funds may not.

Second, let's accept that we are not going to be able to gain access to these strategies for the same price as a Vanguard index fund. These are specialized approaches requiring more brainpower to work and more expense to operate, and we are going to have to pay for them.

Third, let's grant that hedge funds have a *moderate* correlation to regular market indexes. They are not an insurance policy with a guarantee to save us when the market is down.

Hark back to the thrilling days of yesteryear. Remember the credit crisis, when the S&P 500 lost 37 percent of its value in 2008? We do. We still wear the lash marks on our backs. How did hedge funds perform during this period? As you may have heard, they were down a lot as well, about 15 to 19 percent. Certainly a big disappointment to anyone who expected hedge funds to be uncorrelated to the stock market, or who expected them to be up when everything else was coming down. But then, being down 19 percent is better than being down 37 percent.

We mentioned how 2000 to 2009 was called the lost decade for the stock market, which had an annualized return of minus 1 percent over the entire span. Hedge funds had annualized returns ranging from 4 to 7 percent over the same decade.

Gentle reader, hedge fund strategies could be the missing third leg to the stool you are sitting on that is supported by stocks and bonds. While the strategies are miles away from being perfect, they probably represent a meaningful improvement over what you are doing at present. After all, they offer positive expected returns with only moderate correlations to your current holdings. They offer a path to increase your risk-adjusted returns, which means that by using them, you stand to accumulate greater wealth from your investments over time.

Hedge fund strategies could be the missing third leg to the stool you are sitting on that is supported by stocks and bonds.

What's more, because these strategies are less correlated to the stock market, they are less correlated to the rest of your life: your job, your 401(k), your house. They should help—at least relatively—when everything else is riding three cars behind the flowers. Having a meaningful portion of your assets bet on things that aren't disintegrating will help you to stay calm and carry on.

Sometimes people think that using alternative investments such as hedge funds will eliminate risk. That isn't so. Alternative investments simply substitute different risks that pop up in different ways at different times. The effect, however, is that the overall volatility of our portfolios should be lowered. We will be taking more jabs to the body instead of the big haymaker to the skull.

Reality has sharp teeth. Risk means that you can lose money. That's why it's called "risk" and not an ice cream sundae. Just as teenage boys are taught that "No means No," adults need to remember that "risk means risk."

~

Reality has sharp teeth. Risk means that you can lose money. That's why it's called "risk" and not an ice cream sundae.

So, where can we find these investments?

Hedge Funds Meet Mutual Funds

The good news is that hedge funds are going downmarket and coming to a town near you. Greenwich is moving to Main Street.

Essentially, the hedge fund industry has reached the point that the automobile industry arrived at 100 years ago, when Henry Ford put cars onto an assembly line. Cars went from being handmade, one-off products for the elite to mass-produced Model Ts for everyman. The result was a more reliable product, albeit one with less snob appeal.

So, too, with hedge funds. The guts of the hedge funds have been extracted, their DNA has been analyzed and synthesized into the same mutual fund format that retail investors are already familiar with.

The mutual fund format offers tremendous advantages:

- Lower expense ratios
- No performance fees
- Low investment minimums
- Simplified tax reporting
- Daily liquidity
- Daily pricing
- Transparency
- SEC Regulation
- Less leverage

All of which means less risk.

The hedge funds that we read about in the *Wall Street Journal* are outliers: Either they have scored such impressive returns that they merit a headline, or else they are the ones whose directors are being hauled off to prison. Most hedge funds are not so newsworthy. While they have the high-flying image of risky investments, their whole point is actually to reduce risk when used in combination with conventional stock and bond portfolios. They are a strategy of singles, not home runs.

The mutual funds based on hedge fund strategies are new and may feel uncomfortable for that reason, but there is no Bernie Madoff behind the curtain who is going to steal our money. Mutual funds lack that special combination of high leverage and illiquid positions that go to creating a financial Death Star. While the lay perception is that you invest in hedge funds to get rich, for the most part hedge funds have only moderate returns. It's their relatively low correlation to stocks and bonds that lets them add feng shui to the rest of your portfolio.

Master Beta

Of course, as hedge funds have shape-shifted into mutual funds, something is lost in the translation. We have forfeited the possibility of stumbling onto the guy who sees the subprime crisis coming and shorts it and makes us a zillion-aire. Alpha managers like that would want to run a true hedge fund where there was an incentive fee to reward their genius. They wouldn't want to work for a boring conventional mutual fund where performance fees are disallowed.

Like the search for the Lost Dutchman mine or the golden city of El Dorado, the quest for this magic manager has led many investors to ruin, and the sooner we give up looking for him the better off we will be. While we would all love to tap into the bliss of finding a true hedge fund superstar, picking the right manager at the right time, that is not our sport. Instead of dreaming of perfect love, the best answer for most of us is to lower our sights to something more achievable: the returns available from running the generic core of each hedge fund strategy.

From Bogle to Boggle

Let's brush up on some Greek:

- *Alpha*—The extra returns we get from hiring skillful or lucky managers, above and beyond what we could have obtained by investing in an index fund that passively owns the whole market. When we're talking about stocks, an alpha manager is one who beats the S&P 500 index. Unfortunately, there seem to be very few of those chaps around. We always seem to find them just when their hot hand turns cold, which suggests that they weren't unusually skillful to begin with, just lucky for a while.

Because alpha is so rare, we are not going to bother much with it. However, that will not stop us from stretching the term to refer to any excess returns we can scrounge out. For example, we will say things like, "From the point of view of the vanilla stock and bond investor, alternative investments can add alpha."

- *Beta*—The extent that an individual investment responds to swings in the larger market. We are going to use it here to refer to the risks and returns that flow from any specifiable investment strategy. For example, you can access the beta of the stock market by buying an S&P 500 index fund. Since risk and reward are related, you get the standard payout that comes from bearing that standard risk. You buy the stock market, and you get the returns proportionate to owning the market "beta." If you own a portfolio of high beta stocks, you get the risks and returns of the market amplified to that degree. If there is a strategy common to most managers who are running a particular type of hedge fund, we will call this the source of the hedge fund's beta. We are going to casually say things like, "From the point of view of the vanilla stock and bond investor, following hedge fund beta strategies can add alpha."

- *Ouroboros*—A mythical snake that bites its own tail, consuming itself. A word with which you may not be generally familiar. It has nothing to do with finance, but we're going to sneak it into this book anyhow. Watch for it.

- *Quant*—Someone with a Ph.D. in finance from M.I.T. or the University of Chicago. Quants look at the markets abstractly, through the lens of statistical models, and then engineer sophisticated trading strategies (often) using high-powered computers. See also, "Billionaire."

The History of Finance in One E-Z Lesson

Now that we've learned these terms, it's time to start bruiting them about. Since we'd probably get caught if we tried to pass off the following ideas as our own, we might as well admit we cribbed them from AQR Capital's white paper, "Is Alpha Just Beta Waiting to Be Discovered?" Here's a CliffsNotes version (with apologies to Cliff Asness, AQR's head). Hang on to your hat, because it explains the genesis of the alternative investments we are going to be considering throughout the rest of the book.

Financial history illustrates that what we once thought of as excess returns—alpha—has often just turned out to be some investment strategy people were following that had a hidden logic and worked but was not well understood or widely known at the time. Eventually, though, people began to catch on and the formula got out.

In the 1950s and 1960s, if you were a stock market investor, you probably would have held a portfolio of individual stocks that a broker had recommended to you. Everything you earned from this approach could be attributed to your broker's stock picking skill.

Then, with the advance of finance theory and the implementation of index funds, a much tougher bogey emerged. You could separate your stockbroker's performance from that of the market as a whole. A lot of what before had looked like his pure skill could be attributed to the general performance of the stock market. The market was up, he was up. The market was down, he was down.

It gradually dawned on investors that, after expenses, just owning a low-expense, tax-efficient fund that contained every stock in the S&P 500 index was a better way to capture whatever there was to be had from stock market investing. Few stock pickers could beat this index, and no one could tell in advance who they would be. In effect, the stockbrokers' "alpha" had turned into everyday, ordinary "beta" that anyone could get just by buying and holding the whole market.

As academic research into stock market performance continued, alpha retreated further. Certain market anomalies cropped up: Value stocks beat the market, small company stocks beat the market, and low beta stocks performed better than they should for their risks. Managers who specialized in these investing areas naturally outperformed. But then these styles, too were reduced to quantifiable formulae and applied systematically. The alpha managers who survived the indexing cut now had the rug pulled out from under them. Once these style factors were corrected for, there seemed to be precious little alpha left anywhere in the stock market. The quants had fed all the stock market data into their computers and transformed the alpha into beta.

Exiled from the garden, portfolio managers were driven to new pastures in pursuit of alpha gold, but the mathematicians were close at their heels. Almost immediately, the quants turned their sights on to commodities, real estate investment trusts, and emerging market stocks, transforming these exotic alphas into beta.

That is the relentless Hegelian dialectic of investing history: The lawn mower of progress chews up alpha and spits out beta. What first looks like magic turns out to be nothing more than returns that are available by following some specifiable investment methodology. If you don't know the trick, it's alpha. Once you know the trick, it's beta.

The relentless Hegelian dialectic of investing history: The lawn mower of progress chews up alpha and spits out beta.

Today, we stand at a new threshold. Like Ouroboros, the quants have turned the computers on themselves and started digesting their own hedge fund strategies. They have extracted the essence, bottled it into conventional mutual funds, and put them on the supermarket shelf within reach of ordinary retail mutual fund investors.

These alternative betas represent the returns we can achieve by exposing ourselves to the risks shared by hedge fund managers who are pursuing common underlying strategies. To the hedge fund managers, they are beta, but to you and me, sitting on our stocks and bonds, they look like alpha: a source of alternative, low-correlated positive returns.

Far out.

When Phil was in college in California in the 1960s, he came across a book called *Cosmic Consciousness*, which argued that the human race was on the verge of a breakthrough into a higher state of evolution. This finding was reinforced when he saw the mind-expanding ending of *2001: A Space Odyssey*. Unfortunately, nothing much has happened since. We seem to be stuck in the same old low-consciousness place.

On the other hand, investing theory has evolved. The arrival of hedge fund beta for ordinary investors is not to be dismissed. It's not exactly like finding a black monolith on the moon, but it is a small step forward here on the planet of the apes.

The Alternative Reality

Although most of us don't have access to real hedge funds, "lite" versions of their basic strategies are now being packaged inside mutual funds. This represents a giant step forward in the history of investing. Or, maybe it's all hype. We shall see.

Chapter Nine

A Field Guide to Hedge Funds, Part One

~

The Long and the Short of It

WE ONCE MET A PROSPEROUS HEDGE FUND MANAGER AND asked him the secret of his success. He told us that his method is to comb through the newspapers every day, and whenever he reads about a graduate of USC business school being promoted to CEO of a company, he shorts their stock. While this particular strategy is not widespread as far as we can determine, one of the key features that distinguish hedge funds from conventional investments is short selling.

Most mutual funds constrain managers to buy only the stocks they think will go up. Then, under the Taxpayer Relief Act of 1997, the last restriction on short selling in mutual funds was removed, and the result was a spate of new investment products that let investors swing both ways.

This chapter is going to be about those hedge funds whose short selling is central to their strategy. As you have gathered by now, there is not just one type of hedge fund. In fact, there are 10 basic hedge fund types as handed down on the tablets from Dow Jones Credit Suisse. If you want to use somebody else's classification scheme, be our guest. Our plan is to give you a primer on them here and then focus later on some specific mutual funds who run these strategies.

#1. Long/Short Equity

Long/short equity hedge fund strategies purchase securities that the managers believe will rise (the "long" part) in value while simultaneously shorting others that they believe will fall (the "short" part). Put them together and you have long/short equity. Sounds simple, doesn't it? Well, it's not.

What is Short Selling?

Many hedge fund strategies involve shorting stocks and other types of investments. Short selling means selling a security that you don't own, but plan to deliver to a buyer in the future (after the price falls, you hope). In other words, you are betting the price will go down. This sounds un-American, but it is actually a vital part of price discovery. If only long purchases were allowed, the sole way you could express your opinion that the price of a stock is too high would be by standing on the sidelines. Short selling allows you to back your negative opinion with your wallet. Notice that this has the salubrious effect of not letting prices go unreasonably high. The market price represents the consensus of all buyers and sellers for any given security, unlike an auction where only the buyers have a voice.

That's the theory, anyway. No doubt it can be abused when short sellers conspire to set up kill zones and bring their withering crossfire to bear on a single company, but that is a discussion for another occasion.

You short a stock by borrowing the shares you want to sell today from somebody who already owns them (a broker, typically) and then, when you want to close your position (*cover your short*), you buy the shares back on the open market after the price has—you hope—fallen and then you return the shares to their owner. You earn the difference between the cheap price you paid today to replace the stock you sold for the high price earlier (less the transaction expenses).

For example, let's say you believe that the price of Apple Computer (AAPL) is headed for a fall. You borrow 100 shares of AAPL from your broker at $250 a share and sell them today for $25,000. Then, in a few months, everyone catches on to how overhyped Apple's products are, and the price of AAPL falls to $100 a share. You buy the 100 shares back again for $10,000, return them to the broker, and keep the difference—$15,000—less whatever the broker charged you to rent them.

Easy money? Yes, especially if you're right.

On the other hand, what if you're wrong? Then it's not so good.

When you are a long investor, all you can lose is what you initially paid for the company. If you paid $250 a share for Apple, and Apple simply disappears from the map, you are out $250, *finis*. Now imagine that you short Apple by selling 100 borrowed shares today for $25,000, and tomorrow morning Apple holds a press conference announcing that it has perfected the flying car, just like George Jetson used to drive. Ten minutes later, Apple stock rises to $10,000 a share. Your broker calls and says it needs the shares back. Now you have to buy the 100 shares you borrowed back for $1,000,000, leaving you with a loss (before expenses) of $975,000.

The bottom line:

- Long investing—the downside is limited and the upside is unlimited.
- Short investing—the upside is limited and the downside is unlimited.

You may be right about Apple stock being overhyped, but if you short it you can go broke waiting for other people to come to the same conclusion. Being right and early is simply another way of saying that you were wrong.

Being right and early is simply another way of being wrong.

The Long/Short Game Plan

Right away you can see how a fund that can go both long and short has the opportunity to do better than one that is long-only. Your standard mutual fund manager undoubtedly has all kinds of opinions about good and bad stocks, but he is only able to express these opinions by buying the good ones that he thinks are going up. The long-only mandate of most mutual funds ties his hands. To the extent that his opinions have value, he is leaving a lot on the table. However, most long/short hedge funds don't operate so simply. It's usually not a manager buying some stocks and shorting others.

Let's assume the manager has no skill whatsoever. He's just buying and shorting stocks by throwing darts. What will his performance look like?

He is likely to underperform in a rising stock market, since his shorts will drag him back. But he will outperform in a down market, since his random short positions will protect him somewhat from the general decline. If his judgment about the stocks is correct, he will do better, but this is the baseline performance curve he fights every day.

The problem is, there's nothing very hedgy about this. His fund goes up when the market goes up, and down when the market goes down—just not as much either way. Institutions are not going to come rushing to hand this manager their money unless his track record is outstanding. He's selling his performance, but his fund isn't much of a stock market hedge.

What's a long/short manager to do? Something more clever. He might buy small company stocks and short large company stocks. In fact, that is what the typical long/short manager actually does. Or, he might buy value stocks and short growth stocks. He might buy cyclicals and short staples. He might go long India and short China. It all depends on his area of expertise. All his bets could lie within a specific sector, such as technology or financials.

Keep in mind that the holding period for the securities might be measured in minutes. The long/short pairings might have been selected by a computer, based on some statistical properties of their prices. The computer might be buying recent losers and shorting recent winners and waiting for their prices to converge. This is called *statistical arbitrage*. The fund might be engaging in hundreds of these bets at any instant.

Another approach used by long/short managers is *index arbitrage*. As news hits the stock market, not all stocks react equally quickly. A manager could bet on the laggards to follow the leaders. Again, it wouldn't matter if the stocks were going up or down; he could make money for his fund either way by going long or short depending on whether the news was good or bad. This is an extremely tricky proposition for the fleet of mind and execution.

Whatever he does, he can amplify all these trades by using *leverage*—either by borrowing money or by using *options*—contracts that allow you to buy or sell an asset at a prespecified price in the future—on these stocks. Options let him control a large number of shares for a small amount of money. If his bet pays off, the returns are magnified; if it does not, the options expire worthless and he moves on to his next idea.

The hedge fund manager doesn't have to win them all. He just needs a small edge over chance, sufficiently levered to make a respectable profit. It helps to have high speed computers and to pay infinitesimal commissions. This is not something you can do by placing phone calls to your full-service broker.

Because shorting is such a fundamental idea to hedge funds, we had to go long on explanation. Our next ones will be short.

#2. Market Neutral Equity Funds

There are two cousins of the long/short approach that stand as hedge fund types in their own right. Long/short funds like those discussed above can be either net short or net long, depending on the views of the manager. Equity market neutral funds, on the other hand, take their long and short positions in stocks while conscientiously minimizing their exposure to the systemic risk of the stock market.

These funds practice *relative-value fundamental arbitrage*. In other words, they find pairs of stocks with a high correlation to each other and then go long the one they like and short the one they don't. For example, let's say our manager is an expert on the automotive business. He decides that Ford is a buy and GM is not. He buys Ford and shorts GM.

What's interesting about this pair of trades is that the outcome will be unrelated to the stock market at large, and even unrelated to the performance of the automotive segment. The only thing that matters is whether he is right or wrong. If the market falls 1,000 points but Ford does better than GM, he's made money on the trade and he's a genius; if the stock market rises 1,000 points but

Ford does worse than GM, he's lost money and he's a bum. With the stock market taken out of the picture, he is in a safer position to lever up his bet.

In the end, these managers will hold equal dollar weights of their long and short positions.

Market neutral equity funds can be designed to be neutral regarding currency weights, country weights, industry weights, market capitalization weights, or whatever neutrality is of interest. These funds are typically low risk, low return affairs, along the lines of conservative fixed income investments.

So, why would people obsess over this? Because of portfolio theory, which says that adding uncorrelated assets to your portfolio does you a lot more good than adding correlated assets. Most people pile on highly correlated assets (tech stocks, growth stocks, emerging market stocks, foreign stocks) and think they have a diversified portfolio, which they do, right up until the minute they don't. Adding a market-neutral equity fund really diversifies, because it can make money in any economic environment if the manager can make the right calls.

#3. Dedicated Short Bias

Unlike the long/short funds and the market neutral funds, the dedicated short bias funds do just what the title suggests: They maintain a constant net short exposure.

As a result, they will have a negative correlation to the rest of the stock market. For example, anybody who said the stock market was riding for a fall before 2008 was immediately crowned by the press as a far-sighted savant when the crisis hit—even if the reasoning behind their "the end is coming" pronouncement was totally specious. The few who actually did short the market that year made a killing for their investors. Because a dedicated short portfolio has by definition a high negative correlation to the rest of the stock market, these funds will do wonders for a portfolio so long as you can make money investing this way. In a bull market, though, that can be quite a challenge, as they rack up big losses year after year. The managers operate in the bizarro world where beauty is ugliness and everything is upside down. The occasional wins when the market corrects won't be enough to make up for the gaping losses they sustain the rest of the time. We need to remind ourselves here that the long term direction of the stock market is up (it's true). Betting constantly against the market has been a tough way to make money in the United States for the past 200 years.

------------------- ~ -------------------

Betting constantly against the market has been a tough way to make money in the United States for the past 200 years.

Therefore, these funds are better used to express your view that the world is coming to an end, or at least temporarily coming to an end. That kind of call is notoriously difficult to make, because it is really two calls: one to get out of the market and one to get back in, and both calls have to be timed correctly for it to work. Making the right call but getting the timing wrong equals making the wrong call.

Beware—dedicated short bias funds are not to be confused for even an instant with the inverse or leveraged inverse mutual funds and exchange-traded funds marketed to retail investors. Those funds attempt to do 100 percent (or sometimes 200 or 300 percent) of the inverse of some index, such as the S&P 500 index of large U.S. stocks. The problem is, because these funds target the daily price change of the index, it turns out that the series of daily price changes is not at all what you get or expect from, say, the inverse of the one-year price change. In some cases, the stock market can be down and your leveraged inverse fund can be down, too—exactly the opposite of what you expected. These funds work for day traders but few others (and, frankly, we doubt they work for day traders). There is even some question whether these finds might blow up if stressed by extreme circumstances. These funds are complicated, risky, and unnecessary for any but the highest of high fliers. Stay far away from these bad boys.

#4. Global Macro

As the name implies, global macro managers take a 35,000-foot view of the world economy at a macro level and place their bets where they perceive imbalances, relative misvaluations, or other opportunities. With the whole world spread out before them like a land of dreams, they have a wide field to carry out their operations. They can make leveraged bets in equity markets, currency trades, interest rate futures, and commodities, in both developed and emerging markets worldwide. They are free to move wherever they perceive opportunity.

Many global macro managers have a quantitative approach, looking for prices that have moved far from equilibrium and seem poised to regress toward the mean, or for pairs of price movements that appear mispriced relative to each other and so create an exploitable gap. These funds keep especially alert to noneconomic factors, such as central bank policies or political maneuvering, which may distort prices. When something looks out of equilibrium and poised to correct, they pounce.

Perhaps the most common macro ploy is the *carry trade* popularized by Bruce Kovner, who used it as a virtual ATM to manufacture cash for his investors at Caxton

Associates. The idea was that you borrow money from a country with low interest rates (say, yen from Japan), and then lend it at higher interest in another country (say, New Zealand bonds). The trick is that you don't hedge the currency risk, you just rake in the difference between your borrowing cost and what you receive in interest. This works as long as New Zealand dollars don't depreciate relative to the yen.

The most famous trade in global macro history was in 1992 when Stanley Druckenmiller and George Soros realized that the Bank of England did not have sufficient reserves to defend the British pound against devaluation but nevertheless would be stupid enough to try. Their Quantum fund proceeded to sell massive quantities of sterling. The net result was a $1 billion dollar transfer of wealth from British taxpayers to their fund's shareholders, while Britain futilely tried to defend the pound. Not bad for a few days' work.

#5. Managed Futures

Remember when all the other kids were smoking cigarettes and pressuring you to light up? Your parents probably told you that it's a bad idea to go along with the crowd. But in the upside-down world of hedge funds, trend following is a *good* thing. If it weren't for this bad advice from our parents, we might be rich hedge fund managers today. Trend following is extremely trendy in managed futures funds. Like long/short and arbitrage funds, managed futures go both long and short and use leverage. Managed futures are a bit like the commodities funds we discussed in Chapter Six. While a commodity index fund will passively buy and hold a basket of different commodities, managed futures are actively run by commodity trading advisors, or CTAs. These advisors typically have a proprietary system for trading in the futures markets, which include commodities but also trade currency, equity, and fixed income futures markets all over the world. There are over 100 liquid futures markets that can be traded within these asset classes. Some of these commodity trading advisors may be like Eddie Murphy in *Trading Places*, who follows his gut feelings about pork bellies, but more commonly traders use a *trend following* system to guide their buy and sell orders. Some would say "trend creating," but that would be the subject for another book.

Trend following refers to the fact that investors love trends. When they see the market going up they pile in. When they see the market going down they stampede to the exits. It works best when things go from good to great or, interestingly, from bad to worse. It stutters when the market is choppy and directionless.

Note the "bad to worse" part. As hedge fund researchers William Fung and David Hsieh conclude in a 2004 paper, "Trend-following strategies thrive when conventional asset markets are distressed, which provides a valuable diversifying source of return to portfolios of conventional assets." In 2008, when global equity prices were collapsing, managed futures were up sharply. But unlike, say, a dedicated short bias equity fund, they also can make money when the market is going up. Any trend, up or down, is their friend.

There is market psychology at work here. Investors are a notoriously anxious bunch and look for security by copying one another. This groupthink leads to momentum-driven, trend-creating events. The short-term voting machine of the market continuously undershoots and overshoots its long-term fair value.

The short-term voting machine of the market continuously undershoots and overshoots long-term fair value.

There are many ways to try to capture trends. For example, you might look at how prices have been moving for the past 10 days as a short-term indicator, the past 45 days as a medium-term indicator, and for the past

12 months as a long-term indicator. If all of these are moving up (or down), you might conclude that there is a strong trend operating and invest accordingly. If two of the three are moving up, you might conclude that there is a weak trend and take a smaller position, and so on. You can make the formula as simple or as complicated as you want. There is inevitably going to be a certain amount of back-testing and data mining of uncertain reliability and validity in these models.

Of equal importance are the rebalancing and bet-sizing risk management strategies that are superimposed over the trend following system. These managers have to periodically rebalance their portfolios to maintain exposure across each of the 100 or so markets in which they invest. This means that they don't let the trends run forever, but eventually sell some of whatever has gone up to top off whatever has fallen below their baseline position size. In addition, they have to size their positions carefully, adding more weight where the trends appear strongest and placing smaller bets where the evidence is weaker. They don't want to bet the farm on any one prediction, but patiently hope to make money across the totality of their transactions.

Does this really work? The evidence is that these strategies have been used to make money for futures traders since the 1960s. They even have a low correlation to ordinary commodities (0.18 to the Goldman Sachs Commodities Index) over this period. Managed futures have all the appearance of being a friend in times of trouble, the most welcome kind.

In the next chapter, we turn to funds where arbitrage is the principal strategy.

Chapter Ten

A Field Guide to Hedge Funds, Part Deux

~

Arbitrage, et al.

ARBITRAGE SOUNDS HARD, BUT THERE'S LESS TO IT THAN meets the eye.

Let's say Nintendo releases a new game station just before Christmas, and it sells at a huge premium on eBay. However, you notice that Amazon suddenly has inventory at sticker price. You could sell the game boxes on eBay and fill the orders from Amazon, pocketing the difference in price.

A sweet deal, but don't quit your day job. Opportunities for riskless profits are rare and fleeting, since other market participants discover them and attack like piranhas until there's nothing left. That is life under efficient markets. An example in finance might be noticing a difference between the price of gold in London and New York. Or a difference between Berkshire Hathaway's class B and A shares of stock that is more or less than the 1500:1 ratio at which they are supposed to exchange. Arbitrage refers to a transaction involving two similar or fungible items that are priced differently in different markets. An *arbitrageur* is someone who practices arbitrage. Not to be confused with *saboteur*, an agent who blows up bridges behind enemy lines.

As time has passed, the term arbitrage has been watered down to mean taking a long and a short position on similar assets, often with an eye toward locking in a profit from any price discrepancy between the two. Since even this usage is too strenuous, today arbitrage means any nifty trade: the simultaneous buying and selling of two related securities or assets whose prices seem out of sync with each other.

Arbitrage (def.): **a nifty trade.**

Now we are going to look at some hedge fund approaches where arbitrage is their beat.

#6. Convertible Arbitrage

No sooner have we defined one term than we have to crack open Webster's once more: *convertible*. This term means way more than a car with the top down. A convertible bond is really a hybrid security: a conventional bond with an out-of-the-money stock option stapled to it. Think of it as a bond with a split personality.

Here's how it works: When a company's stock is below a certain price, it pays a coupon until maturity just like any other bond. But if the company's stock price rises above a certain threshold, the bond owner can convert the bond into shares of the company's stock. You might say that below the preset stock price, it's a bond; above the price, it's a stock.

The prospect of becoming a stock is what makes the convertible bond appealing. However, it is also appealing for the company that issues it, because it lets them pay a lower rate of interest on the money they borrow than they would otherwise. Therefore, companies issue convertible bonds because it is their cheapest means of raising money. While this sounds like a win-win situation, it is not without risks to the buyer. These companies are usually younger, smaller, and riskier—relative newcomers with great growth prospects but not much financing. They carry with them a higher risk of default, which is why they have to offer the prospect of stock shares as an added inducement.

You can buy a basket of convertible bonds in a mutual fund from Vanguard (ticker: VCVSX). That, by itself, is not a hedge fund. So, how do we promote these bonds into an alternative investment idea? Like this: When a company issues a convertible bond, the hedge fund buys the bond and then shorts the stock of the company.

Stay with us here:

If the stock *falls* in price, the hedge fund makes money from its short position. The value of the bond also falls, but usually less than the stock does because bondholders have better protections in the event of bankruptcy than stockholders do. Meanwhile, the fund keeps the coupons from the bond. The gains from shorting the stock plus the coupons redeemed along the way more than make up for the fall in the bond's price.

If the stock *rises* in value, the short position is self-hedged as the bond is converted into a stock.

What is more, the manager can cover his bases further by using futures contracts to hedge the interest rate risk and credit default swaps to hedge the bond's default risk. What he is left with is a pure play between the value of the sum of the parts (the bond plus the stock option) and the price he paid for the convertible bond when it was issued, which came out at a discount because of its relative illiquidity. The manager got this discount because he supplied capital (liquidity) when it was scarce. He is left with an asset that can be difficult to dispose of thereafter. As Warren Buffett says, writing a check is what separates conversation from commitment. Wired up in this fashion, the fund can make money no matter how the company does, or, for that matter, how the rest of the stock market does. That is what makes it a hedge fund.

Of course, the strategy isn't fail-safe. The value of the bond can fall faster than the stock price. Or, other arbitrageurs can take the profit out by bidding up the price of the bond too high in the first place. If the manager does a lot of these trades, however, diversification pushes the odds in his favor.

#7. Fixed-Income Arbitrage

Fixed-income arbitrage made the headlines when Long-Term Capital Management, the enormous hedge fund run by John Meriwether and Nobel Prize winning economists Myron Scholes and Robert Merton, threatened to take down the global economy when it blew up in 1998.

The idea behind this alternative investment is to exploit mispricings in the fixed-income arena, one of the most relentlessly efficient of all markets. While fixed-income arbitrage encompasses a number of strategies, they basically come down to making bets on the direction of interest rates, changes in the yield curve, credit quality, future volatility, or perceived mispricings within or among the different classes of fixed-income instruments. Admittedly, that's quite a mouthful.

In practice, it is less mysterious. The generic fixed-income arbitrage manager buys lower-credit bonds and then hedges out the interest rate risk by shorting the higher credit quality Treasury bonds at the same maturity. He then banks the higher coupons from his higher-yielding bonds. Or, he identifies a small mispricing based on the historical relationships between the fixed-income securities, takes offsetting long- and short-positions, and waits to profit as the rates converge back to a syzygy (*syzygy*—a harmonious alignment).

How do fixed-income arbitrage managers do this? Let's say we buy a corporate bond and then short a Treasury bond at the same maturity. Changes in interest rates will have no effect on our profits. Our trade gleans the difference between the (higher) coupon on the corporate bond and the (lower) coupon on the riskless Treasury. Of course, if the corporate bond is downgraded, we stand to lose money.

We also might identify mispricings along the yield curve. The yield curve describes the relationship between interest rates and the length of time until a bond's maturity. Typically, short-term bonds pay a lower rate of interest, and long-term bonds pay a higher rate, for all the reasons discussed in Chapter 2. Due to their ready availability, brand new Treasury bonds sell at a slight premium to older "off the run" Treasuries, but the values converge when these bonds are held to maturity. Or, for example, sometimes 5-year Treasury notes might look temporarily cheap relative to 2-year Treasury notes and 10-year Treasury bonds. By buying the former and shorting the latter, we stand to make money if the price corrects according to how our model says it should. We can do the same thing with foreign bonds versus U.S. bonds, or municipal bonds versus Treasuries, or even junior and senior securities of the same company.

Remember, too, that the holding period might be a matter of minutes. While any one trade can be problematic, if trades are numerous and diversified, the risks can be reduced. As long as the manager is right most of the time, the fund makes money.

As these mispricings are typically small, a lot of leverage must be applied to goose the profits along the way. With leverage comes the possibility of losing a lot of money if the markets don't move as anticipated. It's no wonder that fixed-income arbitrage has been described as "picking up nickels in front of a steamroller."

While acknowledging that Nobel-prize winning economists may fish in these waters, we would like to observe that predicting the future direction of interest rates is not an exact science. Our friend, Weston Wellington at Dimensional Funds, recounts how in June 2009 the 10-year U.S. Treasury note stood at 3.52 percent, a yield so low that rates had nowhere to go but up, especially in the context of the government's wild $2 trillion spending program. The *Wall Street Journal* canvassed 50 economists for their views, and 43 of them said the Treasury yield would move higher in the year ahead. But one year later, the yield had fallen even further, to 2.95 percent—even while gold was posting record highs.

              ~

Forecasting interest rates is not an exact science.

Fixed-income arbitrage strategies tend to prosper in calm, benign economic environments, producing stock-like returns with bond-like volatility. However, all these tightly correlated relationships can disintegrate in volatile markets as credit spreads widen—precisely when the hedge would be most desired. This was a major problem during the recent credit collapse.

The rule of thumb is, if you are going to make market prognostications, predict often enough and some of them may work out.

#8. Event-Driven

Back in the day, event-driven managers were gunslingers from investment banking who had a feel for how corporate deals would go down. They might do a few deals at a time with hundreds of millions of dollars riding on the outcome. One of them—Ivan Boesky—was able to use his insider contacts to find out about the deals even before they were announced, which can be extremely profitable . . . before you get sent to prison.

Today, event-driven hedge fund managers scour the news for idiosyncratic corporate events that can create niche opportunities to make money. They look for corporate actions that may result in a change in associated stock prices. Then, they make a close analysis of the situation, carefully estimate the probabilities associated with the different possible outcomes, and size their bets accordingly.

Primarily, event-driven strategies occur when a merger or acquisition is announced (*merger arbitrage*), or when a company is significantly downgraded by a credit ratings agency and appears destined for bankruptcy. Events also include spinoffs, share buybacks, lawsuits, or something as mundane and mechanical as the rebalancing of a stock index.

What does all this mean in practice? Imagine you are the manager of an event-driven hedge fund. One morning while you are having your shoes shined and drinking a latte you read in the *Wall Street Journal* that Worldwide Widgets plans to acquire American Widgets. American Widgets is currently selling for $50 a share, so Worldwide offers $60 a share to make closing the deal a slam dunk. To them it's worth $100 a share, because once they take out the competition from American Widgets they plan to raise prices.

Corporate event ahoy! Returning to the office, you power up your Bloomberg machine to find that the price of American Widgets has already risen to $58 a share, and there it sits. Does this mean you are too late? Not at all. This is where your role as a hedge fund manager begins.

Why hasn't the price risen all the way to $60, the offering price? The answer is, because investors are not certain the deal will go through. Maybe Worldwide will retract its offer. Maybe the Justice Department won't let them merge. Maybe American Widgets doesn't want to be acquired and will put up a fight. The point is, the deal is probable and promising, but by no means a sure thing.

Across town, in a gleaming skyscraper, sits the manager of an ordinary stock mutual fund. By sheer luck, his port-folio contains American Widgets, and in the course of

10 minutes he has watched the stock price rise from $50 to $58. This manager doesn't know whether the deal is going to go through or not. He does know that he can book an immediate profit by selling right now. Or, he can wait and take his chances on getting that extra $2 if the deal eventually closes. Decisions, decisions.

He calls his wife and asks her what to do. She tells him, "What—are you nuts? Cash in that $8-a-share gain immediately. It's going to make your quarterly report look great. Sell!"

But who will buy? The answer is, you will, the fearless event-driven hedge fund manager. In anticipation of collecting the extra $2 in a few months, you are happy to pay $58 today. Note that if the deal falls apart, you immediately stand to lose $8 a share on American Widgets as its price plummets helplessly back to its pre-deal level of $50.

Why would you take such a lopsided risk? Well, your fund contains nothing but these kinds of merger candidates. You figure that not all of them will work out, but most will, and your fund will make money on the balance. You make money by supplying liquidity (cash) to the market at a time when a lot of other people are motivated to sell to lock in a profit. Most people don't want to take a bet that says, if I win I get $2 but if I lose I lose $8. You will, though, because you know that 90 percent of the time these deals go through. Doing just one deal might not be smart, but doing a whole portfolio of deals is.

When the economy is good, there are lots of mergers and acquisitions for the event-driven hedge fund manager to exploit. Prices are bid up and the acquirer's stock has more room to fall. On the other hand, when the economy is bad, deals fall apart and the funds have higher correlations to the market, just when we wish they wouldn't. Merger arbitrage funds tend to have higher correlations to the rest of the stock market than other hedge fund strategies for this reason.

Distressed Securities

Distressed securities are another class of investments of interest to event-driven managers. These are typically bonds of companies that have been downgraded from "investment grade" to "junk" status. The legal mandates of many pension funds and the investment policy statements of many bond mutual funds do not allow them to hold anything but "investment grade" bonds in their portfolios. This leads to a spate of wholesale selling as these bonds have to be unceremoniously dumped onto the market.

For the individual investor, buying these would be a risky proposition. After all, there is a reason the company was downgraded. He could be buying a bond that would soon be in default, risking a near total loss on his investment.

From your point of view as an event-driven fund manager, however, this is another buying opportunity. You already own a bunch of these distressed bonds, all bought at a significant discount. You know some will fail, that's baked into the cookie. But even in bankruptcy, bondholders may be partially paid off from the proceeds. It won't be a total write-off.

Others will stabilize. In some cases, the company may reorganize successfully and their bonds will get upgraded. You can't predict which is going to be which. Since you own a portfolio of these bonds, your risks are diversified. The key to the deal is the bargain price you paid for the bonds as they were being offloaded to the market. The discount you got for providing liquidity when it was scarce more than compensates for the risks, on average. Hedge fund operators are always alert to people buying or selling for other than good economic reasons.

#9. Emerging Markets

This category has nothing to do with arbitrage but we had to put it somewhere.

Emerging markets is the polite term for the underdeveloped countries where 80 percent of the world's population lives. Most of these countries have come a long way, thanks to the growth of global capitalism. Go to Bangladesh today and you don't find as many starving children as in the 1950s; instead, you find shopping centers.

Many emerging economies have good enough legal systems and property rights to merit investment. (After all, the United States was once an emerging market, but graduated to become a developed market and has proved to be one of the great investments of all time.) Even so, investments in emerging markets face higher risks as well as higher rewards than in developed markets.

Since lots of plain vanilla emerging market mutual funds already exist, what does an emerging market hedge fund bring to the table? Not the ability to go short, since short-selling is not allowed in many of these countries. Not the ability to use options or other derivatives to leverage returns, since these may not exist in many of the markets where these funds graze.

What they can do that is different is buy bonds, commodities, currencies, and real estate in addition to stocks. They can take concentrated positions, by industry or by country, based on their research and information edge. Unlike their mutual fund manager counterparts, they can also buy holdings that are illiquid. But whatever they are up to, they do it in the emerging markets.

#10. Multi-Strategy

This catch-all category refers to hedge funds that employ some combination of the nine other approaches just covered. Hedge funds were typically founded by talented money managers who broke off from larger firms to start their own funds in their special area of concentration. As these funds filled to capacity, there came the need to expand their offerings. As a result, groups of managers banded together and started new funds that pooled together their expertise. However, it would be a mistake to think of these multi-strategy hedge funds as some kind of multigrain biscuit made up of hedge funds.

The multi-strategy classification is really just a way for hedge fund sponsors to compete with the middlemen— the hedge fund fund-of-funds. The multi-strategy framework gives managers the flexibility to shift to whatever hedge fund styles are currently working best. Rather than just being random combinations of the other nine strategies, they are often more like market timers who deploy their capital in the target-rich environment *du jour*.

The benefit to the managers is that they don't have to worry that a fund-of-funds will pull the plug the instant their particular specialty runs cold and then watch all their assets walk out the door. The benefit to investors is that they get further diversification among hedge fund strategies, without paying the extra layer of expenses routinely raked off by the fund-of-funds managers (1 percent fees plus 10 percent of the profits, typically, for a hedge fund fund-of-funds on top of the standard fees of the hedge funds themselves). Of course, you have to be satisfied with the submanagers. It's possible that the fund-of-funds could more than make up for their fees if they can pick better managers in each area.

How They Stack Up

Table 10.1 shows how the 10 hedge fund strategies have performed since 1994, with thanks to Dow Jones Credit Suisse for letting us publish it.

Just to walk through the numbers:

- The first row shows the returns and risks of owning the S&P 500 index of U.S. stocks, a common market benchmark. This is what hedge funds are trying to hedge.
- *Mean* refers to the average annual return after expenses of the funds in the Dow Jones Credit Suisse database over the entire time period.
- *Volatility* is the standard deviation of the returns, a measure of risk.
- *Correlation* to the S&P 500 shows how highly the strategy has varied within the U.S. stock market. The values can range from –1 to +1, with zero meaning no correlation. Other things being equal, the lower this number, the better.
- *% of H.F. Assets* refers to how much of the total money invested in hedge funds is currently devoted to each strategy.

Table 10.1   Hedge Fund Strategy Characteristics 1994–2010

Strategy	Mean	Volatility	Correl S&P 500	% of H.F. Assets
S&P 500 Index	8.0%	15.7%	1	NA
Credit Suisse/Tremont Hedge Fund Index	9.4%	7.7%	0.56	NA
Long/Short Equity	10.2%	10.0%	0.65	20.8%
Equity Market Neutral	5.1%	10.6%	0.28	2.2%
Dedicated Short Bias	−3.8%	17.1%	−0.75	0.2%
Global Macro	12.5%	10.0%	0.25	19.6%
Managed Futures	6.6%	11.8%	−0.10	5.0%
Convertible Arbitrage	7.9%	7.1%	0.36	1.7%
Fixed Income Arbitrage	5.3%	6.1%	0.40*	5.0%
Event Driven	10.4%	6.1%	0.62	25.1%
Emerging Market	8.2%	15.2%	0.63*	7.2%
Multi-Strategy	8.2%	5.5%	0.36	13.2%

*Correlation to Dow Jones World Index.

(Continued)

What is our takeaway? All of these strategies, with the exception of dedicated short bias, would have been good additions to our stock portfolios since 1994.

~

Nearly all of these strategies would have been good additions to our stock portfolios.

We note that the most popular strategies are event-driven, long/short equity, global macro, and multi-strategy. This is no coincidence. Money follows success.

Notice, too, how the Dow Jones Credit Suisse Hedge Fund Index of all the funds in their database has good risk/reward properties as well. This gives us the following brainwave: Is there a simple, one-fund solution to gaining hedge fund diversification for our alternative investing portfolios? Let's cut to the chase.

The Alternative Reality

Congratulations! You have now finished your brain boost and everything will be clear to you from now on. You have attained cosmic consciousness.

We have covered the 10 basic hedge fund alternative investment strategies. They are predicated on shorting, providing liquidity, taking on illiquid investments, and generally doing an insane amount of research on recondite topics that funds can exploit to make small amounts of money and then leverage to make very satisfactory amounts of money.

Next stop: reconstituting the core of these strategies into mutual funds.

Chapter Eleven

One-Fund Solutions

Destroy All Replicants—or Not?

UNLESS YOU HAVE VAST PERSONAL RESOURCES AND SKILL in selecting fund managers, real hedge funds are not going to serve as good diversifiers for your portfolio. A friend has a stockbroker who recently recommended a hedge fund to him with an unbelievably great track record. This is exactly the wrong way to proceed. The rule of thumb is that you start with a survey of the field in relation to your needs and then do 75 to 100 hours of research on any hedge fund manager you select.

If you check your piggy bank, you probably don't have enough money to buy all the conventional asset classes plus an extra million dollars apiece to get into a sampling of the 10 different hedge fund strategies. If you have a half-million dollars to throw at this you might invest in a hedge fund fund-of-funds, but you still have to pick the right manager, which means you are back to the 75 to 100 hours of research.

No need to despair if this is not your situation. These new hedge-funds-in-mutual-fund-wrappers are going to provide an alternative.

There are two different methods used by these hedge fund mutual funds. Both try to deliver hedge fund performance, but they arrive at this place following completely different routes.

1. *Hedge Fund Replicants*: A top-down approach to mathematically replicate the returns of hedge fund indexes. We'll call these "hedge fund replicants," which has a nice sci-fi ring to it. They recreate hedge fund returns either using other mutual funds, or by using various combinations of stocks, bonds, commodities, currencies, and so on to get exposure to the set of risk factors they need.

2. *Hedge Fund Strategies*: A bottom-up approach, pursuing the actual hedge fund methodology itself zipped up inside a mutual fund.

We are ready to start naming names.

In this chapter, we call out some funds, first those that are replicants and then those that follow hedge fund strategies. We close by talking about our pitiful efforts to create our own long-only hedge fund.

Hedge Fund Replicants

By analyzing databases of hedge fund performance, math wizards (primarily William Fung and David Hsieh, Harry Kat and Helder Paloaro, Andrew Lo and Jasmina Hasanhodzic) discovered how to clone hedge funds by using ordinary ingredients like those you already have lying around the kitchen. In effect, the quants quantified the quants. Sometimes these replicated funds were used by institutions to give their clients a place to stash their alternative dollars during any interregnum between hedge fund investments.

How did they do it?

———————————— ∽ ————————————

In effect, the quants quantified the quants.

————————————————————————————

It's a little bit technical, but basically the replicants take the data series of hedge fund returns and do a regression analysis to reproduce it using a set of conventional risk factors: so much stocks, so much bonds, so much currencies, so much commodities, so much credit, so much volatility, and Shazam!—they have it. The replicant funds triangulate the hedge fund returns the same way Frankenstein was reverse-engineered from graveyard body parts. They end up with a synthetic hedge fund that mimics the behavior of the real thing—not precisely, but in a way that's good enough for home use.

The formula can be applied to all hedge funds taken as a group, or it can be applied to each hedge fund strategy taken individually. This approach washes out all the idiosyncratic fund manager contributions to the total returns and extracts just that portion attributable to their exposure to common underlying risk factors.

This all sounds sexy until you look under the hood. For example, a hedge fund replicant might contain 40 percent corporate bonds, 20 percent emerging market stocks, 11 percent small cap stocks, and so on—a lot of the same stuff we already own. Of course, it shouldn't matter if it contained two bus tokens, some pocket lint, and a stick of chewing gum, so long as it delivers the goods. As we have seen, most investors are overexposed to one specific risk factor (equity risk) and underexposed to the others.

With that in mind, we begin with some hedge fund index funds that have been spawned by replication. Normally we would like to lead off by showing you a comparison of their performance over the past three years, but these funds are all comparatively new.

ING Alternative Beta

This fund (ticker: IABAX) is a straightforward attempt to capture the beta of the Hedge Fund Research Index (HFRI), an equally weighted composite of more than 2,000 hedge funds. It uses derivatives in various liquid financial market indexes such as equities, fixed income, currencies, and commodities to track the index.

Natixis ASG Global Alternatives

This fund (ticker: GAFAX) is the brainchild of Professor Andrew Lo, head of financial engineering at MIT and pioneering researcher in hedge fund beta replication. What AlphaSimplex Group (the fund managers, the "ASG" in the fund name) brings to the clambake is active risk management. Lo takes the view that investors do not like to lose a lot of money. The fund manages its volatility (i.e., standard deviation) to an 8 percent target, adding either leverage or cash to keep it at this level. Since volatility is generally the enemy of returns, the fund automatically becomes more defensive when the going gets tough, but then adds leverage to increase returns when seas are calm. The fund makes direct long and short investments in about 26 futures and forward positions to capture the hedge fund betas from the Lipper TASS database of 3,000 hedge funds.

Fun, Fun, Funds 'til Her Daddy Takes the T-Bill Away

We interrupt this chapter to bring you the following public service bulletin.

Since we have just started name-dropping some particular alternative mutual funds, we need to pause here and issue a bunch of disclaimers. As we survey the specific mutual funds here and in the chapters ahead, please keep several things in mind.

The funds we suggest tend to be new and have short track records. We don't have a 75-year data series to analyze that would speak for itself. We can only go by what we see: the bland strategy description from the prospectus (probably written by the fund's legal department), the expense ratio, and whatever short-run correlations and returns we can uncover. Even something as straightforward as a fund's expense ratio can be tricky to pin down, since the sponsoring company will often underwrite a large part of a fund's start-up costs in the hope of attracting a self-sustaining pool of money. We wish we had more to go on, but we don't, so we will try to make the best of what we have.

If there is some fund that you love that is not mentioned here, it could be for several reasons. One is that it didn't turn us on. Another is that we overlooked it. Don't ask which. There are many funds out there in fundlandia. We have tried to characterize the ones here accurately and apologize in advance if we have failed in this mission.

Most funds have different share classes available. There are funds with front-end, level, and back-end loads (commissions) as well as funds with no loads. There are investor and institutional classes of shares. We have not listed all the share classes of every fund, but we will typically list one or two. You can look them up if the fund interests you. We will include a little information about each one in the Appendix, and you can dial your web browser to Morningstar.com to learn more.

Which share class you are eligible to buy depends on whether you are investing on your own, through a broker, or through an investment advisor, as well as which custodian holds your account and how much money you have to invest. If you have an investment advisor, sometimes he can get you into institutional class fund shares that have a high stated minimum dollar investment for less than that amount. Sometimes he can't. This isn't a democracy. Not everyone will be able to get into all share classes of all funds.

Many of these funds have short-term redemption fees. Some will even have the dreaded mutual fund marketing fees (known as 12b-1 fees) attached, if they aren't banned by the time you read this. You know how they always say to read the prospectus? This isn't an S&P 500 index fund. Get out a magnifying glass and read the prospectus. It won't be very enlightening, but at least you will be better off than the guy who hasn't read the prospectus.

The conventional wisdom on mutual funds is that the best single screen to use is a fund's expense ratio. Since most mutual funds are delivering a market return net of their expenses, the lower the expenses, the better their return. That is not true here. These funds can have high management fees because these managers are competing with well-paid hedge fund talent (in some cases, the same managers are running both hedge fund and mutual fund versions of the same strategy). The research they use doesn't come cheap. The internal expense ratios for these funds will flip your wig. When funds are operating high turnover strategies and using leverage and passing through dividends on stocks they are shorting, the annual expenses can run to 15 percent or even higher. Most don't have operating expenses this high, but some do. It doesn't mean the managers are taking their Netjets to the Seychelles. This is the price of running the strategy, the cost of doing business in this space. We wish it were cheaper, but it's not.

In the final chapter we will talk about how an investor might integrate all of these alternative investments with the rest of his or her portfolio. For now, consider all these funds we are listing as a starting lineup of *American Hedge Fund Idol* contestants. If your eyes start to glaze over while reading about specific funds, just skip this part and return to it later as your interest sharpens.

We now return you to your regularly scheduled programming.

Multi-Strategy

For readers who can remember as far back as the last chapter, another approach we mentioned for the investor who wants to pick just one hedge fund type is to use a multi-strategy fund. These funds do not try to replicate the entire hedge fund universe, but they pick from several strategies within it.

The first two funds that we recommend rely on the replication approach.

IQ Alpha Hedge Strategy

The Index IQ (ticker: IQHIX) uses a regression analysis to replicate the performance of each of six of the basic hedge fund strategies mentioned previously—long/short, macro, market neutral, event-driven, emerging market, and fixed-income arbitrage—and reconstitutes their performance using off-the-shelf, plain vanilla exchange-traded funds. They then combine the six factors according to their own formula, and apply up to 25 percent leverage to the results. The idea is to be in market directional strategies during periods of low market volatility and then rotate into market neutral strategies during periods of high market volatility. The correlation of this fund to the S&P 500 has been about 0.76 since late 2007.

IQ Hedge Multi-Strategy Tracker

This fund (ticker: QAI) employs the same strategy as IQ's "Alpha" fund above, but without using leverage. This is an exchange-traded fund that anyone can buy or sell without paying a sales load, and it operates with low expenses.

The next group of multi-strategy funds is not trying to track an index or replicate a benchmark. They pursue multiple hedge fund strategies in their own right, working them inside the mutual fund format. As such, their returns can be expected to vary from those of hedge fund indexes in aggregate. We are getting fund-specific returns, not those of a broad index.

iShares Diversified Alternatives Trust

This exchange-traded fund (ticker: ALT) tries to capture fixed income arbitrage, managed futures, and global macro hedge fund strategies. It makes direct investments in futures contracts to achieve its goals, without the further intermediation and expense of using exchange-traded funds.

Natixis ASG Diversifying Strategies

This fund (ticker: DSFAX) uses a half-dozen hedge fund strategies, including macroeconomic, fixed income, and trend following models, and as far as we can tell, it tries to overweight whatever is working best right now. Here the special sauce is correlation management: When the fund's correlation to the stock market rises above 0.25, they short the stock market component until the correlation falls back to 0.25 or below. This is a significantly lower correlation to the market than that embedded in the hedge fund replicants above, and that makes this fund more hedgy. It also manages volatility to a standard deviation of about 12 percent.

Let us pause here and take this in. This fund actively manages two characteristics that are very important to investors whether they know it or not: correlation to the market, and volatility. This means that the fund will (a) not be just another closet stock market index fund, and (b) that it has a pressure valve on top to let off steam when things get too hot. These are exactly the kinds of bells and whistles that ought to make retail investors take notice. This isn't your grandmother's mutual fund. We're starting to use space age materials. If the execution on the strategy side proves to be good as it is on the risk management side, we will be onto something.

All the above are possible one-fund solutions that let you easily add the hedge fund universe to your portfolio. There is one other avenue to consider before we jump into the strategy-specific funds.

Alternative: Roll Your Own Hedge Fund

At the end of 2007, your authors published their classic tome, *Yes, You Can Supercharge Your Portfolio.* Beneath the breathless title was an attempt to introduce Monte Carlo simulation to retail investors, an introduction we believed was overdue.

Almost as an afterthought, we suggested that an investor could create his own long-only, mini-hedge fund just by selecting stocks with a low correlation to the rest of the market. We were even foolish enough to create a shovel-ready 10-stock portfolio to accomplish this. The companies we picked at the time were:

- General Mills
- Pacific Capital Bancorp
- Wesco
- British American Tobacco
- Chesapeake Utilities
- Amerisource Bergen

- Ball Corporation
- Constellation Brands
- Novartis AG
- Enbridge Energy Partners LP

Little did we know at the time that this casual theorizing would instantly be subjected to the slaughter of 2008. With fear and trembling, we peeked back at how this make-believe 10-stock hedge-fund-lite portfolio performed in 2008, and we were crushed to see that it was down fully 14.6 percent. Some hedge, we thought. We were thankful that we at least had the foresight to write that these companies would regress to the mean going forward, but even so they might present something of a hedge.

Upon further reflection, however, we realized that an S&P 500 index fund was down 37 percent for the year, so our little long-only 10-stock portfolio was still about 22 percentage points to the good.

Then we noticed that the Dow Jones Credit Suisse Hedge Fund index was down 18.7 percent that year. We had even managed to beat that—and without being smart, sophisticated, and above all, well-paid hedge fund managers. In fact, for 2008, this portfolio outperformed the Dow Jones Credit Suisse Convertible Arbitrage Index (down 30.6 percent), the Emerging Markets Index (down

29.5 percent), the Market Neutral Index (down 33.6 percent), the Event Driven Index (down 17.5 percent), the Fixed Income Arbitrage Index (down 27.9 percent), the Long/Short Equity Index (down 19.2 percent), and the Multi-Strategy Index (down 23.3 percent). It was trounced by the Global Macro Index (down 4 percent), the Managed Futures Index (up 19.1 percent), and (naturally) by the Dedicated Short Bias Index (up 16.8 percent). Of course, in 2009 it sat there like a log, but it did hedge a bit when it counted.

The fact that our performance was competitive raises an interesting question: does the emperor have no clothes? Can anyone create a long-only stock portfolio that is relatively disconnected from the fate of the larger stock market of which it is a part? Is there another road that gets us to the same place, bypassing the high-priced talent?

Let's revisit how we came up with our 2007 long-only, unlevered mini-hedge fund.

First, we looked for stocks whose price swings were uncoupled from those of the larger stock market.

Then, we eliminated stocks whose price swings were too volatile, whether or not they were correlated with the S&P 500.

Next, we screened for fundamentals: We eliminated companies who didn't have enough daily trading volume to make them readily liquid. We cut those who had recently trimmed their dividends for any reason, as well as those whose payout appeared suspiciously high. We gave the ax to corporations with no earnings. Finally, we struck from the list any whose price/earnings ratio was more than 25, which meant that they were just too expensive for us poor country boys. We made some effort to select from different industries, including food, banking, insurance, tobacco, utilities, medical equipment, packaging, beverages, drugs, and energy. Note that the list is all stocks—no bonds, no commodities, no REITs.

Our final step was to assemble them into an equally weighted, 10-stock portfolio, using the QPP Monte Carlo simulator. Not only did we want the stocks to have a low correlation to the stock market, we also wanted them to have a low correlation to each other, to maximize diversification.

Would we buy this portfolio today? Not a chance. The list needs updating, since the dynamics of the stocks change relative to the market. For example, we would certainly have jettisoned a financial like Pacific Bancorp early on and replaced it with something better.

Here's another change we would make: We would take a tip from Quantext wizard Geoff Considine and add a screen for stocks that do badly under conditions of high market volatility. Volatility rises sharply in times of panic, so stocks tank as volatility spikes. We wanted off that ride.

The same companies tend to come up again and again when we use these screens. Our new portfolio consists of the following. Note, we're still equal-weighting them.

- Flowers Foods
- Kinder Morgan Energy Partners, L.P.
- General Mills
- Ralcorp Holdings
- Abbott Laboratories
- New Jersey Resources
- Northwest Natural Gas
- WGL Holdings
- Family Dollar Stores
- Archer Daniels Midland

This portfolio reads well on paper. It has a low beta, a low volatility, and a low correlation to the market's volatility. It could provide a useful hedge to a conventional stock-and-bond portfolio.

With our luck, these companies will have gone out of business by the time you read this, but here they are anyway. But, in case this doesn't happen, should you buy this portfolio yourself? Only if you understand what you are doing and are willing to monitor all these factors going forward.

Bottom Line: This portfolio would be a satellite to the rest of your holdings. You could use this in conjunction with the other hedge fund strategies, or you could skip this step altogether. We just wanted to show you that lurking within the forest of the stock market were trees that could build a hedge all by themselves.

The Alternative Reality

There are workable one-fund offerings that offer an alternative not only to stocks and bonds, but also to buying a whole slate of individual hedge fund mutual funds. Some of these—replicants—use mathematics to reformulate the performance of hedge fund indexes using other means. Others run a mixture of different strategies inside a mutual fund wrapper. We have seen that it is even possible to create a hedge fund by choosing stocks that behave differently from the rest of the stock market.

However, before we commit ourselves to a particular course of action, we need to survey what else is out there. These would be the mutual funds dedicated to running a single hedge fund strategy.

Chapter Twelve

Hedge Funds Pigs in Mutual Fund Blankets

~

The Mutual Fund Beauty Pageant Begins

"I WOKE UP WITH A PIG IN A BLANKET," laments Martin Mull in his sad song of the same name. How often have your authors felt this same way, at least when reviewing our monthly brokerage statements. The underlying cause is often the same as well: "I drank enough 'til she looked good to me" Mull sings—only in our case, we were drinking Wall Street Kool-Aid. It can happen to anyone. But thanks to this *Little Book*, it won't have to happen to you.

In this chapter, we are going to review some of the mutual funds that have crashed into the alternative space, running the hedge fund strategies we described in Chapters 10 and 11 inside the cozy cocoon of a mutual fund wrapper. We will list some notable ones here, sorted by hedge fund strategy, and then in the next chapter we will give you our picks. That doesn't mean you can snooze through this chapter, though—your picks probably will be better than ours.

Long/Short Funds

In theory, long/short managers have had an easy job recently. All they had to do was go short in 2008 and then go long in March 2009 and they would have made a killing. That one trade would have put them on the cover of *Rolling Stone*. The rest of the time they could have (indeed, should have) played golf. This trick was so simple that no one could do it. Almost all long/short funds lost money over this period.

We hate to keep quoting ourselves, but as we mentioned in Chapter 10, long/short funds are perhaps the most similar to conventional equity funds, in that they rely on individual managers' stock picking and market timing skill. The result is that long-short equity is the most highly populated area of regular mutual funds that are running hedge fund strategies, with about 50 funds from which to choose—so far.

In an effort to give you some flavor of what owning them would be like, Table 12.1 shows their performance during terrible (2008) and great (2009) years for the stock market. Will they stand out over the next few years? We don't know. Nearly all the funds we examined (about 50) have had negative returns lately. Maybe they will do better going forward; we wish them luck. Those listed in Table 12.1 were the best we found.

It also shows their correlation ("r" being the symbol for correlation) to the S&P 500 stock index over this period. Where we are able to present these tables going

Table 12.1   Long/Short Funds—Recent Performance

	r S&P 500	2008	2009	2010
S&P 500 Index Fund	1	−37.0%	26.5%	14.9%
DJCS Long/Short Equity Hedge Fund Index	0.82	−19.8%	19.5%	9.3%
TFS Market Neutral	0.48	−7.3%	16.6%	6.2%
Robeco Long/Short Equity	0.86	−21.3%	80.9%	26.1%
Wasatch-1st Source Long/ Short	0.91	−20.9%	30.1%	9.4%
Highland Long/Short Equity	0.62	−10.5%	18.1%	4.7%
Quaker Akros Absolute Return	0.43	−2.9%	13.9%	2.1%

forward, we will also show the performance of the relevant hedge fund specialty index in the second row of the table. In this case, we are using the DJCS (which here and everywhere and always stands for Dow Jones Credit Suisse) Long/Short Equity Hedge Fund Index.

TFS Market Neutral

TFS Market Neutral (ticker: TFSMX) acts like a long/short fund even though it calls itself market neutral, and that's why we put it in the long/short category. It has a 0.48 correlation to the S&P 500 from 2007 to 2010. If it were really market neutral, that correlation would be closer to 0.00.

The fund has an offbeat strategy. It invests heavily in market niches like closed-end funds, insider buying, and market order imbalances. It has a high expense ratio, but then it's not just another closet S&P 500 index fund, either. If you like it, you'll be unhappy to learn that the fund is closed to new investors as of this writing, although advisors with clients already in the fund can get their new clients in as well.

Robeco Long/Short Equity

The Robeco Long/Short Equity (ticker: BPLEX) fund managed to do about 20 percentage points better than the S&P 500 annually over the past three years at roughly the same level of risk. That level of outperformance is good enough to get everybody's attention (the fund is also closed to new investors but one day it may open again), but it is unlikely to continue. The manager uses a bottom-up approach, screening stocks on valuation, business fundamentals, and the momentum of fundamentals, and goes long or short accordingly. Their recent outstanding performance is in large part due to their decision to load up on unloved financial stocks in 2009.

Wasatch-1st Source Long/Short

Wasatch-1st Source Long/Short (ticker: FMLSX) brings a stock picking approach to the mid- and large-cap universe, using fundamental and technical analysis to identify companies they believe are over- or undervalued.

Highland Long/Short Equity

Highland Long/Short Equity (ticker: HEOAX) has a broad mandate. They are active stock pickers, looking to buy undervalued stocks and short overvalued ones, like everyone else, only they have done it better lately.

Quaker Akros Absolute Return

Akros (ticker: AARFX) only has about $12 million in assets, which is normally too small for us to recommend since the threshold for self-sustaining profitability in a mutual fund is probably closer to $50 million. A trade-off is that this makes it easy to purchase, since it is part of several mutual fund "no transaction fee" supermarkets at the big brokerages. It generates higher taxable income than most, making it a good candidate for an IRA. It is on Morningstar's radar and has already gleaned a 4-star review at this early stage of its life. The manager appears to be a value investor who makes his long and short calls based on company fundamentals.

Table 12.2 gives a snapshot of the *Upside/Downside Capture* of these funds. That is to say, we took a look at how the S&P 500 Index performed over this period, and divided it into up months and down months, of which there were plenty of each. Then we looked at how each fund performed during the up months (Upside Capture) and the down months (Downside Capture), and then at the results combined. What we wanted to see was a high degree of upside capture, a low amount of downside capture, and as high a combined score (which subtracts the downside from the upside) as possible. That is to say, when the market was

Table 12.2   Long/Short Funds—Upside/Downside Capture

	Upside	Downside	Combined
TFS Market Neutral	38%	29%	9%
Robeco Long/Short Equity	133%	69%	64%
Wasatch-1st Source Long/Short	75%	58%	17%
Highland Long/Short Equity	35%	24%	11%
Quaker Akros Absolute Return	13%	11%	1%

going up, we wanted these funds to be going up, and then when the market was going down, we also wanted these funds to be going up. Greedy, aren't we? We felt that this approach was fair because long/short funds are the most similar to conventional mutual funds. We will hold fire on our evaluations until the last chapter, but we put it here in case you want to draw your own conclusions.

Market Neutral Equity Funds

Market neutral equity funds evenly balance their long and short holdings, leaving you with a portfolio whose entire return has nothing to do with the performance of the stock market and everything to do with the skill of the manager picking stocks. In theory, these funds would have a correlation to the stock market of zero and a beta of zero. If the manager is skillful or lucky, the fund should have a small positive return and a small standard deviation. For that reason, most of them are benchmarked not to equities but to 3-month Treasury bills. That's about as conservative as you can get. Market neutral managers try to sterilize their funds from the important dimensions that customarily determine equity performance: size, value, sector, region, currency, and so on.

Table 12.3 shows how some of the leading contenders have stacked up lately. Notice how the hedge funds inside the DJCS Market Neutral Index melted down in the panic of 2008 alongside everything else.

Table 12.3   Market Neutral Equity Funds—Recent Performance

	r S&P 500	2008	2009	2010
S&P 500 Index Fund	1	−37.0%	26.5%	14.9%
DJCS Market Neutral Index	0.34	−40.3%	4.1%	−0.9%
DWS Disciplined Market Neutral	−0.08	6.8%	−2.0%	3.0%
JPMorgan Research Market Neutral	0.13	−0.6%	10.2%	−1.2%
Highbridge Statistical Market Neutral Select	−0.09	10.3%	−4.4%	−3.7%
Managers AMG Global Alternatives	−0.22	4.8%	1.1%	−3.6%
Hussman Strategic Growth	0.07	−9.0%	4.6%	−3.6%

DWS Disciplined Market Neutral

This fund (ticker: DDMIX) ranks the Russell 1000 U.S. stocks along dimensions of price, earnings growth, and market sentiment, and makes offsetting trades to maintain a market-neutral posture while also controlling for the impact of the different market sectors: transportation, utilities, financials, and so on.

JPMorgan Research Market Neutral

This fund (ticker: JMNAX) is quantitatively managed to be market, industry, capitalization, and style neutral, taking long and short stock positions based on fundamental rankings by JPMorgan's analysts.

Highbridge Statistical Market Neutral Select

This (ticker: HSKAX) is a quantitative fund that takes long and short positions in mid- and large-cap equities to deliver market neutral returns across a variety of investment dimensions. It rises or falls based on its stock selection acumen.

Managers AMG Global Alternatives

When we first heard of this fund, we were hoping that the AMG part of the name referred to the same engineering company that soups up Mercedes Benzes, but there is no relationship. Instead, Managers AMG Global Alternatives (ticker: MGAAX) uses a quantitative tactical asset-allocation strategy across global stock, bond, and currency markets. They take long and short positions across, between, and within these asset classes as they perceive relative value opportunities.

Hussman Strategic Growth

This (ticker: HSGFX) is really a long/short fund with an uninspiring recent record—just one that happens to be better than most other long/short funds. Manager John Hussman is an economist with a proprietary market timing model and a cult-like following. His fund can vary from market neutral up to 150 percent long, and unlike the others, this fund is not market neutral by design. However, his stance is conservative, and he remained market neutral even in the face of the 2009 rally. He posts his economic outlook in weekly missives on the Hussman website (www.hussmanfunds.com).

ProShares RAFI Long/Short

This fund (ticker: RALS) is a new offering from Research Affiliates, and has no track record. We include it because we like its methodology.

This fund simply goes long the 20 percent of U.S. stocks that are cheapest in fundamental valuation, and then shorts the 20 percent that appear to be the most overvalued by the same yardstick, balanced by sector. In this way, the fund is making a bet on the long-term out-performance of value over growth, independent of whether the stock market as a whole is going up or down.

Dedicated Short Bias Funds

Dedicated short bias funds bet against the market, rain or shine. If you hold half your money in the S&P 500 and half in a short-bias fund, this is like putting one foot on the accelerator and one on the brake, which means that you will go nowhere and just lose money to frictional expenses. That makes these funds a tough gig for long-term, buy-and-hold investments. You accomplish the same result just by having less invested in the market and holding more cash. That makes it hard for these funds to bring much to

Table 12.4 Dedicated Short Bias Funds—Recent Performance

	r S&P 500	2008	2009	2010
S&P 500 Index Fund	1	−37.0%	26.5%	14.9%
DJCS Short Bias Hedge Fund Index	−0.8	14.9%	−25.0%	−22.5%
Federated Prudent Bear	−0.95	26.9%	−18.5%	−13.2%
Grizzly Short	−0.94	73.7%	−47.2%	−23.2%
Comstock Capital Value	−0.94	54.3%	−31.1%	−20.6%

the hot tub unless you believe the end is coming. Table 12.4 shows the performance of three funds in this space.

Federated Prudent Bear

The Prudent Bear fund (ticker: BEARX) tries to minimize damage during bull markets by going long on undervalued stocks. In addition to shorting the stock market, the fund can hold cash and Treasury bonds and gold.

Grizzly Short

This bear market fund shorts the domestic stock indexes as well as particular large-cap stocks that appear to be most vulnerable to correction. It may be more convenient for solo retail investors since it can be bought without a sales load.

Comstock Capital Value

Comstock Capital Value (ticker: DRCVX) does not call itself a bear market fund, but it had a correlation of −.93 to the S&P 500 for the past three years. The fund follows a value-oriented strategy, and while it has had a bearish orientation lately, that could switch quickly if the manager's view changes.

Global Macro

Global Macro is a very broad class of hedge funds that pretty much can do anything they like. The "global" part means they can do it anywhere.

Recently, Global Macro hedge funds have not fared well, as illustrated by famous macro manager Stanley Druckenmiller's exit from the business after a disappointing 2009 and 2010. Table 12.5 shows some of the mutual funds that try to work this territory.

PowerShares DB G10 Currency Harvest

Powershares DB G10 Currency Harvest (ticker: DBV) passively executes the "carry trade." It goes long and

Table 12.5   Global Macro—Recent Performance

	r S&P 500	2008	2009	2010
S&P 500 Index Fund	1	−37.0%	26.5%	14.9%
DJCS Global Macro Index	0.31	−4.6%	11.6%	13.5%
PowerShares DB G10 Currency Harvest	0.75	−28.3%	21.2%	−0.7%
Marketfield	0.90	−12.9%	31.1%	14.3%
Eaton Vance Global Macro	0.37	1.7%	10.8%	4.5%
IQ Hedge Macro Tracker	NA	NA	NA	4.5%

short 3-month currency futures to capture the spreads among the different developed-market currencies. Specifically, it goes long the three highest-yielding currencies and sells the three lowest-yielding currencies, usually levering the difference times two. The gimmick behind the carry trade is that higher-yielding currencies have historically tended to maintain their exchange rate against lower-yielding currencies, giving investors a free ride (but with notable exceptions along the way).

Marketfield

Marketfield (ticker: MFLDX) expresses its macro views primarily through equities and long exposure. This means it doesn't "hedge" as much as some other funds in its peer group. As you can see from Table 12.5, it was down 13 percent in 2008 but climbed 31 percent in 2009.

Eaton Vance Global Macro Absolute Return

Eaton Vance Global Macro (ticker: EAGMX) employs the macro toolkit in the bond market, with reasonable expenses and good performance. This is a fund that would do better if housed in your IRA, as it generates a lot of income taxed at ordinary rates (or at least it has recently). The fund is closed to new investors but Eaton Vance has launched a very similar new fund (ticker: EGRAX) that may prove of interest.

Mars Hill Global Relative Value

Mars Hill (ticker: GRV) is a new exchange-traded fund and does not track any particular index. The managers confine themselves to taking long and short positions using a country's exchange-traded funds. In that respect, it is more like a long/short fund. However, its global focus and country versus country smackdown also gives it the flavor of global macro.

IQ Hedge Macro Tracker

The IQ Hedge Macro Tracker (ticker: MCRO) is a hedge fund replicant that targets the Dow Jones Credit Suisse Global Macro and Emerging Market indexes, weighted 50-50. They do an ongoing regression analysis to determine which combination of conventional exchange-traded funds would have most closely tracked this hybrid of the two hedge fund indexes. The fund is not following any particular hedge fund strategy, just looking into a rear-view mirror and simulating what fund managers in these two areas have been doing lately. Research by Hasanhodzic and Lo suggests that global macro is a style amenable to this approach; emerging markets, less so.

Managed Futures

Here are some funds that package managed futures for the rest of us. We could not get specific tax information for these funds, but we suspect that their high turnover might make them good candidates for tax-deferred accounts. Nearly all these funds are new (Rydex being the exception), so we don't have a table of data to present on their recent performance. Depending on which index you follow, managed futures were up between 13 and 18 percent in 2008, a year when commodities and stocks fell 37 percent. Moreover, managed futures have been up more than 10 percent during each of the five worst quarters for the stock market since 1985. That, plus their low correlation to stocks, bonds, and commodities, puts this alternative asset class on your short list.

Direxion Commodity Trends Strategy

The Commodity Trends Strategy Fund (ticker: DXCTX) tracks the performance of the Standard & Poor's S&P Diversified Trends Commodity Trends Indicator. This index offers exposure to 16 commodity markets in 6 sectors and holds them long or short according to the price trends in relation to a 7-month moving average, rebalanced monthly.

Elements S&P CTI

If you are looking for a managed futures fund that tracks the S&P Diversified Trends Commodity index, you can get it cheaper by using the Elements S&P CTI exchange-traded note (ticker: LSC) with its 0.75 percent expense ratio versus 1.93 percent for the Direxion fund above. The exchange traded note format would make for better tax treatment inside a taxable account (at least, unless the IRS rules otherwise). This is not an insignificant benefit, since managed futures funds can be tax-intensive. The downside is counterparty risk with its issuer, the Swedish Export Credit Corporation.

Rydex|SGI Managed Futures Strategy

The Rydex fund (ticker: RYMTX) tracks the S&P Diversified Trends Indicator, which is just like the Commodity Trends Indicator used in both funds above except that in addition to commodities, half the index is weighted to financial futures—primarily currencies from developed and emerging markets as well as U.S. T-bonds and T-notes. It is more expensive than those offerings but offers broader diversification.

Arrow Managed Futures Trend Fund

The Arrow Managed Futures Trend Fund (ticker: MFTFX) attempts to capture price trends in commodities, currencies, and interest rates, but tracks the Trader Vic's index instead. This does not refer to the swank 1960s restaurant famous for its rum drinks with paper umbrellas, but rather an index developed by commodity trader Victor Sperandeo.

Mutualhedge Frontier Legends

Mutualhedge's (ticker: MHFAX) approach is to do due diligence and select five diversified Commodity Trading Advisors to run the money. The fund will rise and fall with the CTA selections it makes. In the unlikely event that the CTAs succeed in squelching competition from the other mutual funds on this list, as they would love to do, this fund will be the only game in town (until someone opens another one).

ASG Managed Futures Strategy

AlphaSimplex Managed Futures (ticker: AMFAX) does not license any index, but uses its own trend-following formula to capture the managed futures beta. It is managed to maintain a target standard deviation of 15 percent. It holds long and short positions in futures and forward contracts in the areas of global equity, global bonds, commodities, currencies, and interest rates.

AQR Managed Futures Strategy

AQR Managed Futures (ticker: AQMNX) also does not license any index, but uses its own proprietary trend-following model. AQR's Cliff Asness wrote his doctoral dissertation on momentum investing. This fund invests in a portfolio of futures and futures-related contracts using more than 100 instruments across four major asset classes: commodities, currencies, fixed income, and equities.

Convertible Arbitrage

As discussed in Chapter 11, you may recall that a convertible bond is an ordinary bond bundled with a call option on the company's stock, which gives the investor the right to convert the bond into shares of the stock in the happy event that the stock price goes up enough. Convertible arbitrage hedge fund managers buy these bonds at a discount when they are issued, supplying the company with badly needed capital. Then they hedge out the interest rate risk of the bond and short the underlying stock. This covers their bet while they wait for the bond to mature, at which point it is redeemed at its full face value.

There are only a few mutual funds that practice this technique (so far), and they are all hybrid offerings that combine convertible arbitrage with other approaches. Here is one—we'll get to some others later. Table 12.6 shows its recent returns.

Table 12.6   Convertible Arbitrage—Recent Performance

	r S&P 500	2008	2009	2010
S&P 500 Index Fund	1	−37.0%	26.5%	14.9%
DJCS Convertible Arbitrage Index	0.59	−31.6%	47.4%	11.0%
Calamos Market Neutral Income	0.96	−13.3%	13.8%	4.9%

Calamos Market Neutral Income

This fund (ticker: CVSIX) combines convertible arbitrage with a "covered call" strategy. Just as we were not crazy about the "buy/write" funds, which seemed to produce the same returns as a stock plus cash portfolio, we are not big fans of covered call funds, either. These funds buy a stock portfolio and then sell call options on the stocks for extra cash. This leaves us with a portfolio that has nearly all of the downside of the stock market with only part of the upside, since if the stock market goes up, the stocks will be called away. The convertible bond and covered call portfolios are not mutually hedging, because when the stock market is down the convertible bonds can also suffer.

In other words, this looks like a convertible bond arbitrage fund with a stock portfolio attached. While John Calamos is a highly-regarded convertible manager, our preference is to find funds that leave us to dial in the stock market exposure we want.

Fixed-Income Arbitrage

Fixed-income arbitrage attempts to exploit small mispricings in the bond market. Table 12.7 shows how some of their mutual fund cousins have performed recently. As you can see, there has not been exactly a *Who*-concert-like stampede of fund managers to get into this area.

Table 12.7   Fixed-Income Arbitrage—Recent Performance

	r S&P 500	2008	2009	2010
S&P 500 Index Fund	1	−37.0%	26.5%	14.9%
DJCS Fixed Income Arbitrage Index	0.63	−28.8%	27.4%	12.5%
Forward Long/Short Credit Analysis	NA	NA	46.5%	4.2%
Western Asset Absolute Return	0.66	−14.8%	32.9%	8.1%

Forward Long/Short Credit Analysis

Forward Long/Short Credit Analysis (ticker: FLSRX) is a relatively new fund that invests primarily in higher-yield municipal bonds and hedges out the interest rate risk by shorting Treasuries of the same maturity. It also takes long and short positions using corporate bonds within the same industry.

Western Asset Absolute Return Institutional

Western Asset Absolute Return (ticker: WAARX) has no benchmark and a broad mandate that allows it to seek returns from fixed income investments however and wherever it can generate them. Their description of their strategy could scarcely be more generic: "The Fund's flexible investment strategy enables the managers to seek opportunities for enhancing total returns through investing in a wide variety of fixed-income securities around the world."

Notice that in both cases the funds have not been market-neutral relative to the S&P 500 Index: They were significantly down in 2008 and significantly up in 2009. One final piece of advice: Fixed-income funds generate a lot of taxable income. Your net returns will be between 1 and 2 percent higher every year if you can park them in an IRA or other tax-qualified account.

Event-Driven

Event-driven hedge funds seek securities that are mispriced relative to each other and whose price is expected to converge due to some corporate event. Merger or risk arbitrage is the most common example.

Unlike in the case of Fixed-Income Arbitrage, there are a number of worthwhile funds in this space, as Table 12.8 points out.

Arbitrage Fund

The Arbitrage Fund (ticker: ARBFX) is actively managed in pursuit of the merger arbitrage. The managers attempt to add value by specializing in smaller companies where

Table 12.8   Event-Driven Arbitrage—Recent Performance

	r S&P 500	2008	2009	2010
S&P 500 Index Fund	1	−37.0%	26.5%	14.9%
DJCS Event-Driven Index	0.76	−17.7%	20.4%	12.6%
Arbitrage Fund	0.39	−0.6%	10.2%	1.4%
Merger Fund	0.52	−2.3%	8.5%	3.4%
Gabelli ABC Fund	0.77	−2.6%	6.0%	4.1%

they hope to find fewer participants and hence more upside. They avoid hostile takeovers, deals where the financing is in question, and those facing significant regulatory hurdles.

Merger Fund

The Merger Fund (ticker: MERFX) is another actively managed merger arbitrage fund. Each proposed deal is examined on its strategic merits, the only question being: Is it likely to close? If they believe it will close, they proceed. This fund may also invest in corporate reorganizations and corporate bonds, but the bread-and-butter of their operations is risk arbitrage.

Gabelli ABC Fund

Gabelli ABC (ticker: GABCX) has a good long-term track record and has the lowest expense ratio in the group, which means more of its returns are passed on to the investor. The main strategy seems to be merger arbitrage, although there is talk of its value and income investing style in the fund literature, so possibly manager Mario Gabelli is running a hybrid. Its numbers make it look a lot like the other merger arbitrage funds, though.

IQ Merger Arbitrage ETF

The IQ Merger Arbitrage (ticker: MNA) is a new exchange-traded fund that pursues a passive, rule-based strategy of buying into all announced mergers that meet its broad criteria. It offers the distilled merger arbitrage beta unlinked to manager performance, and for a low expense ratio. If the fund can't find enough deals to invest in, it parks its money in short-term bond ETFs. Several caveats, though: They short the deals through inverse index funds and even ultra inverse index funds (which we hate) rather than through the specific stock. Also, daily volume (5,000 shares a day at this writing) and total assets ($30 million) are not as high as we would like. That may change by the time you read this.

AQR Diversified Arbitrage Fund

The new AQR Diversified Arbitrage (ticker: ADANX) is a hybrid convertible arbitrage plus merger arbitrage offering brought to you by the supersmart Goldman Sachs refugees at AQR Capital. It is managed to deliver the beta of these two arbitrage strategies.

Emerging Markets

Apart from the IQ Hedge Fund Tracker mentioned above (ticker: MCRO)—a hybrid Global Macro/Emerging Markets strategy replicant—there are presently no mutual funds that execute emerging market hedge fund strategies. Emerging market hedge funds have more in common with a conventional emerging market equity fund such as you might buy from Vanguard (ticker: VWO) or iShares (ticker: EEM), which explains why the correlation between the emerging market hedge fund index and the ordinary emerging market index fund is high, on the order of 0.80. The resourceful investor could supplement an emerging markets index fund with a dash of PowerShares Emerging Markets Sovereign Debt (ticker: PCY) or iShares JPMorgan USD Emerging Markets Bond (ticker: EMB) and have this territory pretty well staked out in his conventional portfolio.

The Alternative Reality

In this chapter, we presented mutual funds that are running hedge fund strategies and caught our attention. For every fund we have listed, there are probably 10 others that we either forgot or that didn't turn our heads. If a fund tweaks your interest, your next stop would be Morningstar.com to glean what you can, followed by a visit to the sponsoring company's website to read all you can about it.

Having reviewed some of the mutual fund offerings that are crashing into the hedge fund space, in the next chapter we talk about the ones we prefer and how they might be integrated into the rest of your portfolio.

Chapter Thirteen

Adding Alternative Investments to Your Portfolio

Finding Your Portfolio's G-Spot

THE TIME HAS COME TO PUT THE 1,000-PIECE PUZZLE together. Having been to the big city and seen the bright lights of Wall Street, it's time to go back to the farm, sit by the stream, and soberly reflect.

As you read this *Little Book*, you may have noticed that some of the alternative investments discussed are complicated. Some of the alternative investing strategies can be difficult to understand. Even if you pore over the mutual fund's prospectuses, you will often find a lot more legal boilerplate and bland generalities than detailed explanations of investment policy.

When it comes to night driving, we are admonished not to drive beyond our headlights. This is a good rule when it comes to alternatives as well. Do not invest deeper than your understanding. Do not invest in them a lot if you only understand them a little.

Don't invest beyond your headlights.

In that respect, these alternatives might be likened to a collectible. There is the ever-present possibility for a serious hobbyist in many fields to make some money by leveraging his time and intellectual effort. If investing for you is a serious hobby, these alternatives can be worthwhile. Even if it turns out that you didn't do much better than you would have with a vanilla indexed portfolio from Vanguard or Fidelity, you will at least have enjoyed the study and learned something along the way. If you end up making some good calls that enhance your risk-adjusted returns, so much the better.

With this in mind, we're going to share our ideas on how to incorporate these alternative strategies into your existing portfolio.

Our first great idea is: Do nothing at all. Just because an investment idea exists, it does not mean that you have to chase after it. The idea needs to persuade you that it is better than what you are already doing.

Here's something else to remember: Incredible as it sounds, we might be wrong. Do your own analysis. You are playing with real money and people can get hurt. We have given the matter some thought but your thinking may be better than ours. This is our snapshot from the early innings.

Our conclusions are probably of less interest than our process in arriving at them, so we are going to share our reasoning, if any. In approaching our recommendations, we wanted to avoid the tiresome game of picking actively managed mutual funds based on their recent performance. We've been around that block twice and didn't like it either time. We also have to weigh the possible desirability of having exposure to an alternative asset class against the fact that we have to choose from a very limited palette of offerings. It might be the case that having an undistinguished Global Macro manager is better than none at all. Or, it might be the case that having no exposure is better. These are judgment calls.

Our Final Exam

Let's revisit the tough, gritty questions we posed at the beginning of this book: Do these approaches work? Are their returns reliable? Are they sustainable or will they disappear? Do they hedge? Do they add value to a portfolio?

There is less agreement that these approaches deliver a return premium than there is about the stock market or the bond market. Still, most investment professionals would agree that these approaches provide an alternative source of returns that should diversify a portfolio and improve its risk-adjusted returns. While no style is in favor all the time, the returns are reliable to the extent that a fund follows a consistent discipline within its domain. Ideally, the fund manager is a quant who stops in the office each morning to turn on the computer, but also sticks around to make sure that what the computer is saying makes sense. What we want to avoid is a guy watching *Mad Money* and going with his gut. That might or might not deliver good returns, but it would not deliver alternative beta.

The performance of these funds could diminish over time as each investment space gets more crowded. There is currently an amount approaching $2 trillion chasing these quarks of opportunity, and they are not infinitely scalable. If there were $6 trillion pursuing the same strategies, their returns could be cut significantly. For the present, a lot of this money is going into long/short equity strategies. These managers are making stock picks. This approach can be scaled up quite a bit. Convertible arbitrage, on the other hand, is a niche market that can get crowded more easily. We have to admit that there have been many market anomalies or occult market risk factors that have existed for decades and continue to reward investors despite all the money poured into them—the value premium, or the small company premium, for example. Hedge fund returns may turn out to be more robust relative to cash inflows than people expect.

Additionally, some opportunities exist not in spite of efficient markets but because of them. Here is an example from hedge fund manager Andrew Redleaf: Every day your bank sorts thousands of pennies into rolls. Some of those pennies might be quite valuable to a coin collector. Nevertheless, your banker does not take time to examine each penny under a magnifying glass to see if it might be worth hundreds or even thousands of dollars. The good and bad pennies all get rolled up together into a tube priced at 100 pennies to the dollar.

The coin collector, on the other hand, is happy to examine pennies looking for that 1909-S VDB Lincoln cent that will make him rich. But just as it does not make economic sense for the banker to spend his time looking at pennies, it does not make sense for the rare coin dealer to take deposits and make loans. They are both profit-maximizing agents, but the banker in the normal course of his activity leaves an opportunity on the table for the coin dealer. The big fish has a big mouth that necessarily leaves some scraps for the little fish.

The hedging properties of these funds vis-à-vis the stock market indexes are less than we would wish and possibly they are lessening over time. Over the last five years, hedge fund correlations to the S&P 500 index have hovered in the 0.70 range—about what you might expect from, say, emerging market equity funds. Yet everyone still diversifies into emerging market funds. The fact that they don't deliver as much diversification as we want is not an argument against getting as much diversification as we can. This is true even where that diversification can be relatively expensive to obtain, as it is with these funds.

Our plan is to walk through how a traditional investor might use alternatives, and then push this all the way to how a new-school, risk-diversified investor would apply them. Interestingly, even a large allocation to most of these alternatives should not by itself be unusually risky. By employing alternatives, we are diversifying our risk exposure. If we put a lot of our portfolios into them, we might lower our risk profiles significantly. But how many of us are in a position to put a large portion of our wealth into relatively new (to us) and untried (by us) strategies? For most of us, a smaller allocation would make more sense, at least initially. With a smaller allocation comes a smaller amount of protection.

In other words, at the levels that most of us will be using them, alternatives will not save us from the next crisis. But they should help. If they improve our risk-adjusted returns in small ways, across an investment lifetime this can make an important difference.

We'll wade into the lake one step at a time, so you can judge for yourself where your comfort level lies.

Conventional Alternatives

If you are a conventional investor with 60 percent of his assets in stocks and 40 percent in bonds (or some similar ratio), the first thing to consider is: Have I maximized the returns from my baseline portfolio?

Then ask yourself the following questions:

- Am I invested in global equities (U.S., foreign developed, and emerging markets), with anywhere from 30 to 60 percent of my assets parked abroad?
- Am I passively accessing the returns from these markets using low-expense, tax-efficient index funds?

- If I am tweaking my stock portfolio, am I tilting it in ways that have historically demonstrated long-term, risk-adjusted outperformance, such as by overweighting small company, value, and low beta stocks?

- On the fixed income side, am I keeping credit quality high and maturities short?

- Do I have a stash of cash put away so that I can sleep at night through the next (personal or national) financial crisis?

- Am I saving regularly so that I can fund my retirement?

- Do I have enough life insurance to take care of my family and keep my wife in candy bars, magazines, and nylon stockings after I'm gone?

If so, you'll be a Man, my son.

No, what we meant to say is, the above checklist is the place to start. Once you have these questions scratched off, it makes sense to think about further diversification. If you are unemployed and sitting around watching TV all day with $30,000 in revolving credit card debt and you haven't made a mortgage payment in six months, there are more important places to begin. The last thing you need to worry about is alternative investments. That fact that you are even reading about them suggests that you are in denial. You need to wake up and smell the coffee (and we mean the breakfast beverage, not the commodity).

If you are unemployed and sitting around watching TV all day with $30,000 in revolving credit card debt and you haven't made a mortgage payment in six months, you have more important things to do than worry about alternative investments.

Assuming that the rest of your financial house is in order, and that you have understood the gist of this book if not the fine points of all the strategies, and you want to take a next step, here is what we would propose.

We want to lay out three ways to go. The first is for an investor with less money, less investment experience, who is self-managing and wants to take a step in this direction. The second is for an investor with more money, more investment experience, who possibly uses the guidance of an investment professional, who has some experience with alternatives and wants to take a bigger step. Finally, just for completeness, we will sketch what a risk-parity portfolio including hedge fund strategies might look like.

Regardless of your profile, we do not recommend that you jump from one end to the other—from a 60/40 portfolio to a risk-parity portfolio—in a single bound unless you have had a long talk with your therapist about it. You should probably begin with a small allocation to alternatives, and then build on this over time as you gain a feel for how they work and then, based on your understanding and appreciation of them, decide whether you want more.

There is rarely any point in making drastic or sudden moves with your portfolio. The paradox is that the more conservative you are, the more you can allocate to alternatives. But this has to be tempered by the psychological imperative of understanding and being comfortable with what you are doing.

A sensible initial move for all investors, if you haven't done so already, would be to lop about 10 percent from the equity side and put it into commodities and REITs. That is to say, if you have 60 percent of your portfolio in stocks, then take 10 percent of that—which is 6 percent (do the math)—and invest it in commodities and REITs. Three percent in each wouldn't be a bad place to start, using low-expense index funds like those we mentioned in Chapters 6 and 7. This brings us to a point where we can consider adding the hedge fund strategies.

The Hedge Fund Couch Potato Portfolio

Having diversified into commodities and REITs, the next step would be to take an additional 10 percent of our portfolio and put it into hedge fund strategies. If our fundamental stance is a 60/40 portfolio, we could take 6 percent for alternatives. If we want to lower our risk profile, we could take the whole 6 percent from the equity side (since equities are typically the more risky asset). If we want to keep a level of risk and return similar to what we have now, we could take 3 percent from stocks and 3 percent from bonds.

What funds would we recommend?

Strange to say, we are not as wild about the replication funds that deliver hedge fund beta by tracking a general hedge fund index as we would like to be.

Here's why not: When it comes to the composite hedge fund indexes, the correlations between them and the stock market are too high for our taste. In other words, these funds can be seen as a bundled sale of an ordinary stock index fund plus the hedge fund index's attempt to add a low correlated, positive return. This means that we are paying high fees for the embedded stock index fund, which we could buy separately from Vanguard for next to nothing. It also means we are paying a lot for the uncorrelated part that constitutes the thin slice of hedge fund salami that we really want. These costs are a meaningful hurdle for an investment vehicle whose expected returns are in the mid-single digits.

Our whole point in making this alternative investment allocation is that we want it to be *alternative*. We already own a stock market portfolio. We don't want to buy it all over again at high expense. We would prefer that the companies who package these funds deliver the alternative beta piece without the stock market sidecar that everyone already owns anyway.

For this reason, for a one-fund solution (if that is what you want), we prefer a multi-strategy fund like Natixis ASG Diversifying Strategies, which has both its volatility and its correlation to the equity market actively managed. The retail class shares (ticker: DSFAX) have a low dollar minimum but carry a sales load, while the Y shares (ticker: DSFYX) are cheaper but you will need an investment advisor to obtain them due to the high minimum.

However, if you have as little as $6,000 to devote to hedge fund strategies and want to get your feet wet, here are some suggestions for getting started .

Event-Driven: In this category, we like the Merger Fund (ticker: MERFX) or the Arbitrage Fund (ticker: ARBFX). Both have a $2,000 minimum purchase requirement.

Confidence Level: Moderately high, surprisingly. While both funds are actively managed, the managers have a long tenure and work within a circumscribed domain, buying the targets and shorting the acquirers in corporate mergers. Domains like merger arbitrage are narrow and there is generally only a small difference among manager performances.

Global Macro: Global macro is difficult to automate and usually relies on the insights of the particular active manager. However, the Powershares DB G10 Currency Harvest Fund (ticker: DBV) captures the currency side (the "carry trade") of global macro passively and efficiently. This is a beta factor to which most investors are underexposed. Just remember that DBV sends out a K-1 to shareholders every year, and your life will be simpler if you hold this fund in a tax-deferred account.

Confidence Level: High. It looks to us like DBV could be—indeed, it probably is—run by a computer.

Managed Futures: When it comes to Managed Futures, we recommend the Elements S&P Citi ETN (ticker: LSC), which uses a trend-following system to go long and short on commodities. It has relatively low expenses of 0.75 percent annually. Among all the hedge fund strategies, managed futures have especially good diversifying properties and tend to show up for us in times of need.

Confidence Level: High. The fund should extract the beta of commodity trends, for good or evil.

These three funds give us access to some core alternative/hedge fund strategies at reasonable expense. Take our proposed allocation to hedge funds, divide it by 3, and put one-third of the money into each one (in this example, that would be 2 percent of your total portfolio into each fund). This gives us a straightforward, set-it-and-forget-it baseline exposure to the hedge fund alternatives.

A Deeper Dive

Research by Ibbotson Associates suggests that while the most conservative investors should be all in cash and the most aggressive investors all in stocks, most of us who fall in between can allocate 15 to 25 percent of our portfolios to hedge fund strategies without batting an eye. We might condense this insight by just taking whatever we are doing and adding 20 percent to hedge fund strategies. This is in addition to the allocation already made to commodities and REITs.

Where should this 20 percent come from? Again, if we want to stay about where we were before on the risk/return continuum, take 10 percent from the stock side and 10 percent from the bond side. If we want less risk (at the price of lower expected returns), we could take the whole 20 percent from the equity side. If we want to make a shift toward higher risk and returns, we would take the 20 percent from the bond side.

With this understanding of how much to allocate, which strategies should we invest in and how much should we put into each?

Multi-Strategy: For do-it-yourselfers, there is the new iShares Diversified Alternatives Trust (ticker: ALT). This fund delivers three hedge fund strategies: fixed income arbitrage, managed futures, and global macro. If you buy it inside an IRA you can probably avoid filing a K-1 partnership form for tax purposes.

For those with an investment advisor, we like Natixis ASG Diversifying Strategies Fund (ticker: DSFYX), as we have already mentioned. The Natixis fund has a higher risk/return profile than the iShares fund does, which is fine by us.

Confidence Level: Moderate. Even though ALT is new, it has a low expense ratio of 0.95, no benchmark, and pursues strategies that historically have low correlations to the S&P 500. We love that DSFYX is directly correlation-managed to make sure its correlation to the S&P 500 does not climb above 0.25. Both funds also actively cap their volatility (standard deviation), a nifty feature.

Long/Short Equity: Long/short equity generally relies heavily on individual manager skill, going long and short stocks according to the manager's judgment. Here we like the TFS Market Neutral (ticker: TFSMX) for both retail investors and those with advisors. Yes, it's actively managed and has an expense ratio of 2.5 percent, but it has delivered the goods. It is closed to new retail investors as we go to press, but some advisors can get you in. Our fallback would be Quaker Akros Absolute Return (ticker: AARFX).

Confidence Level: Just fair. These are bets on active managers, albeit quantitatively minded ones in the case of TFSMX.

Market Neutral: In this category, we like the new ProShares RAFI Long/Short fund (ticker: RALS), and several additional ones for investors with advisors: DWS Market Neutral (ticker: DDMSX) or JPMorgan Research Market Neutral (ticker: JPMNX), or Managers AMG Global Alternatives (ticker: MGAIX). We like Research Affiliates because it operates passively to capture durable market misvaluations at reasonable expense.

Confidence Level: Medium. These funds are quantitatively driven so there may not be a high degree of individual manager risk (or benefit). The ProShares fund has just opened and daily volume and total assets are currently low, but we would expect these to pick up by the time you read this. In other words, don't just put in a market order for 100,000 shares and go to the movies. If this fund operates as intended, it could quickly be promoted to our coveted couch potato hedge fund portfolio pantheon above.

Dedicated Short Bias: Although hedge fund investors in aggregate devote 0.3 percent of their assets to this strategy, we suggest that you invest 0.3 percent less than this, or 0.0 percent. We don't see that the strategy adds value, either historically or theoretically. Until somebody figures out how to deliver returns when the market is down without surrendering returns when the market is up, we would pass here.

Confidence Level: High. It's easy to be confident when you're not recommending anything.

———————————— ∾ ————————————

Although hedge fund investors in aggregate currently devote 0.3 percent of their assets to dedicated short bias funds, we suggest that you invest 0.3 percent less than this amount, or 0.0 percent.

Global Macro: This is an area where there can be a lot of individual manager variability, to which we are constitutionally allergic. We would just as soon stick DB G10 Currency Harvest Fund (ticker: DBV) for the currency carry trade piece and/or the hybrid Global Macro/Emerging Market IQ Hedge Macro Tracker (ticker: MCRO) to bag some of what the hedge fund managers here are getting. With MCRO, remember that trading volume is still thin. Don't place orders large enough to impact the price.

Confidence Level: Good. These are passive, mechanical strategies, and we like 'em that way.

Managed Futures: Along with the Elements S&P Citi ETN (ticker: LSC) already mentioned for the couch potato investor, we recommend the AQR Managed Futures Fund (ticker: AQMIX) or the just slightly more expensive Natixis ASG Managed Futures Fund (ticker: AMFAX). These last two funds go beyond commodities to use their trend-following system across the whole range of futures markets, which is why we prefer them.

Confidence Level: High. AQR and AlphaSimplex are at the head of the class.

Fixed-Income Arbitrage: There is a short list of offerings in this group. We mentioned the Western

Asset Absolute Return Fund (ticker: WAARX) and the Forward Long/Short Credit Analysis institutional shares (ticker: FLSIX) in Chapter 12, but you'll need an investment advisor to get either one. Why do we like them? Our pathetic answer would be because recent performance has been fairly good, and in the case of Western Asset, the expense ratio is low at 0.80.

The alternative—recommending a fund whose recent performance has been bad—seems even less appetizing. However, we would just as soon skip the category altogether until something more appealing comes along. If you do wade in here, remember that these funds are tax intensive and you will be happiest if you find a home for them inside your IRA.

Confidence Level: Unknown to us. We would prefer a fund that mechanically captures the beta of fixed-income arbitrage across a number of strategies.

Event-Driven + Convertible Arbitrage: In this hybrid category, we like the AQR Diversified Arbitrage Strategy Fund (ticker: ADAIX). You will need an investment advisor to get in due to the high minimum investment. This fund takes down two hedge fund strategies with a single blow. Otherwise, consider the Merger Fund or the Arbitrage Fund above, but recognize that they won't deliver the convertible arbitrage part.

You could also add to those the Calamos convertible arbitrage fund (ticker: CVSIX), but recognize that this fund is diluted by the covered-call fund attached to it.

Confidence Level: High. AQR eats hedge fund beta for breakfast.

Emerging Markets: The only offering in Emerging Markets is the IQ Hedge Macro Tracker (ticker: MCRO), which is a replicating hedge fund that also targets Global Macro. If you already own emerging market equities, we think that's close enough, but we also like this fund in the Global Macro arena, so it may be worth having the emerging markets along for the ride.

Confidence Level: High, and we'll like it even better when it has more assets under its belt and a higher daily trading volume.

Okay, there are some picks. How do we hook them up to our chariot?

After lots of fiddling with the dials, the least dumb approach we can think of is to weight them equally. That is, we take the total dollars we are planning to invest in these hedge fund strategies, and divide by the number of strategies we are employing. To make things even simpler, we could just divide our money among the number of funds we are using.

We could get fancy using some kind of historical or risk-adjusted correlated weightings for each strategy, but that is too clever. We are not able to implement each strategy perfectly. We are often relying on one manager's idiosyncratic take on the strategy. In Platonic philosophy, you might say we are dealing with images of images. It doesn't make sense to try to optimize this: we are only optimizing noise. Let's get some meaningful exposure to a mixed bag of hedge fund strategies and call it a day.

A self-managing retail investor could allocate his money equally among the following, giving him access to five or six different hedge fund strategies.

- Multi-Strategy: ALT
- Long/Short: AARFX
- Market Neutral: RALS
- Global Macro: DBV or MCRO
- Managed Futures: LSC
- Event-Driven: MERFX or ARBFX

An investor using an investment advisor could allocate his alternative investment dollars among the following seven funds:

- Multi-Strategy: DSFYX
- Long/Short: TFSMX

- Market Neutral: RALS or DDMSX
- Global Macro: DBV or MCRO
- Managed Futures: AQMIX
- Convertible Arbitrage: ADAIX
- Event-Driven: ADAIX

Please note: Unlike with the simple three-fund solution above, if you are picking a bunch of individual funds to track hedge fund categories, someone needs to monitor them. This should be an ongoing hobby of yours, or you should work with someone who manages money in this territory.

The Portfolio of the Future

Back in Chapter 2 we talked about how equity risk dominates the typical 60/40 portfolio, and suggested that the portfolio of the future might be budgeted according to its risk exposure. The problem was and is that a risk-balanced portfolio using only stocks and bonds would have such a high percentage of bonds that its expected return would be far lower than from a conventional 60/40 portfolio. AQR Capital has recently launched its Risk Parity Fund (ticker: AQRNX) that offers an even exposure to the risks of stocks, inflation, and the term and credit risks of bonds. Their solution is to use leverage to bring the returns back up to those expected from a 60/40 portfolio.

Figure 13.1   A More Risk-Diversified Portfolio (Dollar Weights)

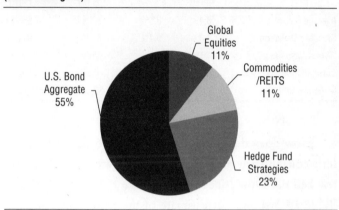

Another possible way to address the problem is to add more asset classes. By Phil's calculations—and reasonable men will disagree—a four-way risk-balanced portfolio would look something like Figure 13.1.

This new industrial-strength hedge fund allocation could be divided equally among the six or seven funds just mentioned. In this portfolio, the risks are budgeted approximately 25 percent to stocks, 25 percent to term and credit, 25 percent to inflation-sensitive assets, and 25 percent to alternatives. These risks are not completely uncorrelated, nor could they ever be, but they are considerably more spread out than they would be in the standard 60/40.

Table 13.1   Portfolio Comparison 1995–2010

	60/40	6% H.F.	20% H.F.	Risk Parity
Average Return	8.4%	8.5%	8.7%	7.9%
Standard Deviation	9.8%	9.1%	8.7%	4.9%
"Worst Case" Year	−31%	−28%	−26%	−12%
Correlation to S&P 500	0.99	0.98	0.97	0.76
$1 Grows to	$3.36	$3.44	$3.56	$3.30

How does this portfolio stack up? To figure this out, let's conveniently assume that our hedge funds would have tracked the Dow Jones Credit Suisse Hedge Fund Index. Table 13.1 shows our estimate of the risks and returns of these portfolios from 1995 to 2010, after expenses.

Table 13.1 starts with the 60/40 stock/bond portfolio, and as we go across the columns from left to right, it adds 6 percent in hedge fund strategies, then 20 percent in hedge fund strategies, and ends with the tribal rock-love risk-parity portfolio shown in Figure 13.1.

The risk-balanced investor on the far right of the table has less drag from the volatility baggage that the 60/40 investor is carrying on the far left. He has decoupled his life to a considerable extent from the vicissitudes of the stock market—a good thing. He will lag his neighbors when the stock market skyrockets, but he will sleep more soundly when it crashes. It looks as if it gives us a big slice of the returns of the 60/40 portfolio with considerably less risk.

Importantly, the risks and returns won't show up at the same time. There will be times when the 60/40 portfolio performs a lot better and we will feel like chuckleheads for being more diversified in a risk-parity portfolio. If the disparity in performance becomes great enough, we will be tempted to run back to stocks. But a prerequisite to embracing more deviation from the Dow is the responsibility to stay the course at such times. This implies sufficient self-knowledge—truly a rare-earth element—to know that we won't punch the eject button at exactly the wrong time.

We are not, repeat not, suggesting that you drop everything and put all your money into a risk parity portfolio. We just want to put it out there to stimulate your thinking. This is the path that alternative investments take you toward, and it is one closer to the way many institutional portfolios are managed.

The Alternative Reality

There are going to be more alternative funds coming out. How can you evaluate them? Are you just supposed to sit on your hands waiting for Stein and DeMuth to write another book? Possibly . . . but not necessarily.

(*continued*)

The Alternative Reality, *continued*

You may have noticed that some companies seem to specialize in providing funds in this area. AQR Capital and AlphaSimplex seem to have well thought out implementations of hedge fund strategies; any new offerings from their laboratories deserve scrutiny. If Dimensional Funds ever move into this space (we hope they do and doubt they will), we would be quick to put their funds on a short list to review.

For retail investors, Index IQ has created a number of hedge fund replication indexes and we expect more funds to come out from people who license their indexes.

We also expect that there will be more individual offerings from hedge fund managers going retail. Mutual fund ranker Morningstar is always on the lookout for these strategies and is more likely to review even a relatively new fund if it is in this area. Your authors occasionally kick around the idea of starting a fund-of-funds themselves to provide a one-stop diversification into these alternatives. If and when we ever do—and believe us, that day may never come—we will post a notice on the dazzlingly high-tech Stein-DeMuth website (www.stein-demuth.com).

Conclusion

Quest into the Unknown

WE HOPE THAT YOU HAVE FOUND THIS *BAEDEKER* GUIDE to some of the new alternative investments to be informative and understandable. Whether or not you decide to invest in them, by now you should have more knowledge to back your course of action. You will also be less mystified the next time someone brings this stuff up at the water cooler or on business TV, and less inclined to invest in something you shouldn't. The last thing Wall Street wants is an informed consumer. Now that person is you.

The financial services industry has been flat-footed in its response to the financial crisis of 2008. Their business model is to sell stocks when the market is good and then hide under the desk when they come tumbling down. Then, repeat. They are very good at selling stocks and stock funds, as well as any fancy products that have a high commission or internal fee structure. That is their comfort zone—what they know how to do, and what they do.

However, not everyone has been asleep. Some very smart people have been quietly at work trying to intelligently design a better investment mousetrap. Financial instruments are being engineered to systematically diversify risk and to expose people to sources of risk and return beyond those of stocks and bonds. Important investment parameters are being actively managed in real time, parameters such as risk exposure, total volatility and the correlation to equity markets.

The new products are more complicated than a stock fund. They give lie to the "simpler is better" adage that worked impeccably under the old investment paradigm but does not apply here. Because they are more complicated to run, they cost more to administer, which means they also violate the "cheaper is better" rule. That rule gives almost perfect guidance when it comes to straight stock and bond investing, but this is a brave new world.

These products should help people build wealth over time. Why? Because they don't put investors on a roller coaster where they consistently jump on near the top of a market because it's so much fun and everyone else is doing it, but then jump off at the bottom because they have lost a lot of money and are afraid of losing everything.

This saves investors from the repeated and gigantic "buy high, sell low" maneuvers that do more than anything else to destroy their wealth. These mild-mannered instruments moderate and distribute risk so investors can stay on for the whole ride and collect the whole return. They deliver more wealth because they provide more peace of mind.

These new alternatives are few in number and difficult to recognize because they are in the soup with thousands of other investment products vying for our attention. They won't make anybody's year-end list of 10 hot stocks that are set to pop. They don't grab headlines. However, if they work in the field the way they do on the whiteboard, better-engineered products will gradually become the core of most smart investors' portfolios, exactly as index funds have replaced active stock picking (and with the financial services industry dragging its feet the whole way). If they work as intended, the next stage of investing will belong to Clark Kent and not to Superman.

Appendix

Fundamentals

HERE IS SOME INFORMATION ABOUT THE ALTERNATIVE funds we have mentioned in the book. These figures can change without notice, so please check with Morningstar .com or the fund company for the latest. We have not mentioned all share classes of all funds but have listed a representative sample.

Hedge Fund Beta

ING Alternative Beta

Name	Ticker	Load	ER	Minimum
ING Alternative Beta A	IABAX	5.75%	1.40%	$1,000
ING Alternative Beta I	IIABX	None	1.15%	$250,000

Natixis ASG Global Alternatives

Name	Ticker	Load	ER	Minimum
Natixis ASG Global Alternatives A	GAFAX	5.75%	1.60%	$2,500
Natixis ASG Global Alternatives Y	GAFYX	None	1.35%	$100,000

Multi-Strategy

IQ Alpha Hedge Strategy

Name	Ticker	Load	ER	Minimum
IQ Alpha Hedge Strategy Inv	IQHOX	None	1.96%	$2,500
IQ Alpha Hedge Strategy Inst	IQHIX	None	1.95%	$250,000

IQ Hedge Multi-Strategy Tracker

Name	Ticker	Load	ER	Minimum
IQ Hedge Multi-Strategy Tracker ETF	QAI	None	1.13%	None

iShares Diversified Alternatives Trust

Name	Ticker	Load	ER	Minimum
iShares Diversified Alternatives Trust	ALT	None	0.95%	None

Natixis ASG Diversifying Strategies

Name	Ticker	Load	ER	Minimum
Natixis ASG Diversifying Strategies A	DSFAX	5.75%	1.70%	$5,000
Natixis ASG Diversifying Strategies	DSFYX	None	1.45%	$100,000

Long/Short Equity

TFS Market Neutral

Name	Ticker	Load	ER	Minimum
TFS Market Neutral	TFSMX	None	2.50%	$5,000

Robeco Long/Short Equity

Name	Ticker	Load	ER	Minimum
Robeco Long/Short Eq Inv	BPLEX	None	2.75%	$2,500
Robeco Long/Short Eq I	BPLSX	None	2.50%	$100,000

Wasatch-1st Source Long/Short

Name	Ticker	Load	ER	Minimum
Wasatch-1st Source Long/Short	FMLSX	None	1.34%	$2,000

Highland Long/Short Equity

Name	Ticker	Load	ER	Minimum
Highland Long/Short Equity A	HEOAX	5.50%	2.24%	$5,000
Highland Long/Short Equity Z	HEOZX	None	1.89%	$5,000

Akros Absolute Return

Name	Ticker	Load	ER	Minimum
Akros Absolute Return	AARFX	None	1.99%	$2,000

Market Neutral

DWS Disciplined Market Neutral

Name	Ticker	Load	ER	Minimum
DWS Disciplined Market Neutral S	DDMSX	None	1.66%	$2,500

JPMorgan Research Market Neutral

Name	Ticker	Load	ER	Minimum
JPMorgan Research Market Neut A	JMNAX	5.25%	1.48%	$1,000
JPMorgan Research Market Neut Sel	JMNSX	None	1.23%	$1,000,000

Managers AMG Global Alternatives

Name	Ticker	Load	ER	Minimum
Managers AMG Global Alternatives A	MGAAX	5.75%	1.91%	$2,000
Managers AMG Global Alternatives Inst	MGAIX	None	1.48%	$1,000,000

Highbridge Statistical Market Neutral

Name	Ticker	Load	ER	Minimum
Highbridge Statistical Mkt Neut A	HSKAX	5.25%	1.92%	$10,000
Highbridge Statistical Mkt Neut Sel	HSKSX	None	1.68%	$1,000,000

Hussman Strategic Growth

Name	Ticker	Load	ER	Minimum
Hussman Strategic Growth	HSGFX	None	1.05%	$1,000

Proshares RAFI Long/Short

Name	Ticker	Load	ER	Minimum
Proshares RAFI Long/Short	RALS	None	0.95%	None

Dedicated Short Bias

Federated Prudent Bear Fund

Name	Ticker	Load	ER	Minimum
Federated Prudent Bear A	BEARX	5.50%	1.72%	$1,500
Federated Prudent Bear Instl	PBRIX	None	1.49%	$1,000,000

Grizzly Short

Name	Ticker	Load	ER	Minimum
Grizzly Short	GRZZX	None	1.49%	$10,000

Comstock Capital Value

Name	Ticker	Load	ER	Minimum
Comstock Capital Value A	DRCVX	5.75%	2.06%	$1,000
Comstock Capital Value AAA	COMVX	None	2.06%	$1,000

Global Macro

PowerShares DB G10 Currency Harvest

Name	Ticker	Load	ER	Minimum
PowerShares DB G10 Currency Harvest	DBV	None	0.75%	None

Marketfield

Name	Ticker	Load	ER	Minimum
Marketfield	MFLDX	None	1.81%	$25,000

Eaton Vance Global Macro Absolute Return

Name	Ticker	Load	ER	Minimum
Eaton Vance Glbl Macr Absolute Return A	EAGMX	4.75%	1.00%	$1,000
Eaton Vance Glbl Macr Absolute Return Inst	EIGMX	None	0.71%	$250,000

Mars Hill Global Relative Value

Name	Ticker	Load	ER	Minimum
Mars Hill Global Relative Value	GRV	None	1.49%	None

IQ Hedge Macro Tracker

Name	Ticker	Load	ER	Minimum
IQ Hedge Macro Tracker ETF	MCRO	None	1.13%	None

Managed Futures

Direxion Commodity Trends Strategy

Name	Ticker	Load	ER	Minimum
Direxion Commodity Trends Strategy Inv	DXCTX	None	1.93%	$2,500

Elements S&P CITI ETN

Name	Ticker	Load	ER	Minimum
Elements S&P Citi ETN	LSC	None	0.75%	None

Rydex|SGI Managed Futures Strategy

Name	Ticker	Load	ER	Minimum
Rydex|SGI Managed Futures Strategy A	RYMTX	4.75%	2.05%	$2,500

Arrow Managed Futures Trend Fund

Name	Ticker	Load	ER	Minimum
Arrow Managed Futures Fund A	MFTFX	5.75%	2.00%	$5,000
Arrow Managed Futures Fund C	MFTTX	None	2.75%	$5,000

MutualHedge Frontier Legends

Name	Ticker	Load	ER	Minimum
MutualHedge Frontier Legends A	MHFAX	5.75%	2.20%	$2,500
MutualHedge Frontier Legends C	MHFCX	None	2.95%	$2,500

Natixis ASG Managed Futures Strategy

Name	Ticker	Load	ER	Minimum
ASG Managed Futures Strategy A	AMFAX	5.75%	1.72%	$2,500
ASG Managed Futures Strategy Y	ASFYX	None	1.47%	$100,000

AQR Managed Futures Strategy

Name	Ticker	Load	ER	Minimum
AQR Managed Futures Strategy Inv	AQMNX	None	1.50%	$5,000
AQR Managed Futures Strategy Inst	AQMIX	None	1.25%	$1,000,000

Convertible Arbitrage

Calamos Market Neutral Income

Name	Ticker	Load	ER	Minimum
Calamos Market Neut Income A	CVSIX	4.75%	1.14%	$2,500
Calamos Market Neut Income	CMNIX	None	0.89%	$1,000,000

Fixed Income Arbitrage

Forward Long/Short Credit Analysis

Name	Ticker	Load	ER	Minimum
Forward Long/Short Credit Analysis Inv	FLSRX	None	1.93%	$4,000
Forward Long/Short Credit Analysis Inv	FLSIX	None	1.57%	$100,000

Western Asset Absolute Return Instl

Name	Ticker	Load	ER	Minimum
Western Asset Absolute Return Instl	WAARX	None	0.80%	$1,000,000

Event-Driven

Arbitrage Fund

Name	Ticker	Load	ER	Minimum
Arbitrage R	ARBFX	None	1.63%	$2,000
Arbitrage I	ARBNX	None	1.38%	$100,000

Merger Fund

Name	Ticker	Load	ER	Minimum
Merger	MERFX	None	1.41%	$2,000

IQ Merger Arbitrage ETF

Name	Ticker	Load	ER	Minimum
IQ Merger Arbitrage ETF	MNA	None	0.77%	None

Gabelli ABC

Name	Ticker	Load	ER	Minimum
Gabelli ABC	GABCX	None	0.66%	$10,000

AQR Diversified Arbitrage

Name	Ticker	Load	ER	Minimum
AQR Diversified Arbitrage Inv	ADANX	None	2.69%	$5,000
AQR Diversified Arbitrage Inst	ADAIX	None	2.46%	$5,000,000

Emerging Market/Global Macro

IQ Hedge Macro Tracker

Name	Ticker	Load	ER	Minimum
IQ Hedge Macro Tracker ETF	MCRO	None	1.13%	None

Acknowledgments

YOUR AUTHORS WOULD LIKE TO GRATEFULLY EXPRESS OUR appreciation to the people who helped bring this book to life: our agents, Lois Wallace (Ben) and Robert Diforio (Phil); our Wiley editor, Debra Englander, and development editor, Kelly O'Connor. Without their continual exertions on our behalf, you would now be staring at a blank page.

About the Authors

Ben Stein can be seen talking about finance on Fox TV News every week and writing about it regularly in *Fortune* magazine, *The American Spectator,* and *Newsmax.* Not only is he the son of the world-famous economist and government advisor Herbert Stein, but Ben is a respected economist in his own right. He received his B.A. with honors in economics from Columbia University in 1966, studied economics in the Graduate School of Economics at Yale while he earned his law degree there, and worked as an economist for the U.S. Department of Commerce. He taught law and economics for many years at Pepperdine Law School.

Ben Stein is known to many as a movie and television personality, especially from *Ferris Bueller's Day Off* and from his long-running quiz show, *Win Ben Stein's Money*. But he has probably worked more in personal and corporate finance than anything else. He has written about finance for *Barron's* and the *Wall Street Journal* for decades, and was a columnist for the *New York Times* for many years. He was one of the chief busters of the junk-bond frauds of the 1980s, has been a long-time critic of corporate executives' self-dealing, and has written numerous books about personal finance. He frequently travels the country speaking about finance in both serious and humorous ways, and is a regular contributor to the *CBS News Sunday Morning*, Fox News Network, and CNN. He was the 2009 winner of the Malcolm Forbes Award for Excellence in Financial Journalism.

Web site: www.benstein.com.

Phil DeMuth was the valedictorian of his class at the University of California at Santa Barbara in 1972, and then took his master's in communications and Ph.D. in clinical psychology. Both a psychologist and an investment advisor, Phil has written for the *Wall Street Journal*, *Barron's*, the *Journal of Financial Planning*, and *forbes.com*, as well as *Human Behavior* and *Psychology Today* (or anybody who will publish him), and is co-author of eight books with Ben Stein. His opinions have been quoted in *Yahoo! Finance*, *On Wall Street*, and *Fortune* magazine, and he has been profiled in *Research* magazine and seen on *Forbes on Fox*, *Wall Street Week*, and various CNBC shows (basically, anybody who will have him). All this pales before his major achievement, which was when Phil's high school rock band opened for *Herman's Hermits* at the Steel Pier in Atlantic City. Today Phil runs Conservative Wealth Management LLC in Los Angeles, a registered investment advisor to high-net-worth individuals, institutions, and foundations.

Web site: www.phildemuth.com.